Lead,

Lead, Follow, or Get Out of the Way

Tales of Survival from the Corporate Battlefield

Gail E. Hamlin

ISBN : 1-4196-5203-6

To order additional copies, please contact us.
BookSurge, LLC
www.booksurge.com
1-866-308-6235
orders@booksurge.com

Lead, Follow, or Get Out of the Way

Table of Contents

Acknowledgements

This book was made possible by the efforts of so many people. For over twelve years I had countless experiences that contributed to the overall meat of this book. To those that I reported to over the course of my career and everyone that I've brushed shoulders with down in the trenches: Thank you!

I'd also like to thank my Mom, Rob, my Schmoopy; Donna, Andrea, Kim, Pam, Everton, Dewi, Razz, Michelle, Aziz, Roger, and everyone who really helped me move this project along. This would not have been possible without the input and support of those that contributed their stories and words of wisdom. If they don't all have new jobs and better bosses yet, then I hope that they do shortly!

Introduction

<u>Lead, Follow, or Get Out of the Way: Tales of Survival From the Corporate Battlefield</u> is indeed based on real experiences gained by working in the corporate world. Many of these experiences belong to others and some are taken from my twelve year journey through Corporate Hell. In order to protect everyone (the innocent as well as the guilty), I've changed all names and the most distinguishing details. Any representation to real people – whether you *think* it's you or someone you *think* you know - is purely coincidental. Besides, if you see yourself as one of these bat-$#@%-crazy managers that I make examples of, then you have larger issues than thinking I've written about *you*. Besides, there are people far and wide that have these same tales to tell. Listen to what people are saying about their bosses in these stories and think about your words and actions. I'm holding up a mirror, folks. If you don't like what you see then it's up to you to take the steps to make changes for the better.

That said, this book is intended to provide accurate information with regard to the subject matter covered. However, I accept no responsibility for inaccuracies or omissions. Furthermore, I specifically disclaim any liability, loss, or risk, whether personal, financial, or otherwise, that is incurred as a consequence, directly or indirectly, from the use and/or application of any of the contents of this book. Enjoy.

Keep in mind as you peruse through the tales and the management lessons associated with them, that I am not a licensed therapist nor am I a lawyer. Please do not think I am. I don't even play one on TV. I am not engaged in rendering legal, medical, counseling, or other professional services or advice by publishing this book. My tales are largely for entertainment. I do not claim to have all the answers. I can only tell you what I did (or what someone else did) in certain situations. If you have a mind of your own, you'll be able to decide what you're comfortable with.

My corporate career spanned twelve years. During my incarceration in corporate America I crossed paths with all kinds of people. This book is mostly inspired by the misfits I used to call Boss. Of course, there are some ragtag coworkers I should thank too. Really, this book has been made possible by so many different people. Don't get me wrong; there have been many, many people I met and worked with along the way that have been inspirational in a good way. It's just unfortunate that none of those people were MY managers.

Following in my father's footsteps (ok, more like kicking pebbles along the sidelines), I chose a career in media. It was a good profession with a promising future if I worked hard and played my cards right. Mistakes inevitably happen, and I'm no different. I certainly made my share along the way. It was on this journey that I discovered what I liked to do and what I didn't like to do. I'm a big believer in doing what I want to do. Right there was my first mistake in the corporate world. *You do not count*. Anything you say or do will be used against you. You know the cliché, "It's a jungle out there"? Well, I've worked with my fair share of monkeys. Don't get me wrong; as I've mentioned, I also had opportunities to work with some of the brightest individuals in the industry. But this book isn't about them.

In life, there are basic principles to live by. For almost every activity that people participate in, there is some guideline to follow, some rule, however complex or simple. Business is no different. As a matter of fact, there are many principles that affect how business is conducted.

Some of the best words of wisdom I've read were written by Robert Fulgham, author of *All I Ever Really Needed to Know I Learned in Kindergarten*. Chapter One outlines these principles as I've adapted them to good management practices. These principles, or commandments as I call them, are based on lessons learned during childhood. However, childhood was a long time ago. So consider this a refresher course. Again, I make no claim that this will work. In order for any of these ideas to work everyone involved would have to have some common sense as well as half a brain to know that it isn't about them. So leave your egos at the door for someone else to stomp on and get on with it.

I started this book as a blog in order to get me into the habit of writing again and to prepare me for writing a book. It began as a daily rant. Then I started throwing other bits of research in as well as others' stories. Then a small following developed. Then a newsletter. Now the book. This book encapsulates the experiences and lessons learned as originally laid out in the blog (Self-Helpless: True Stories of a Working Girl). Leave a comment or just say Hi.

So before you begin reading the first chapter, I want to take the time to thank you for buying my book. Each book I sell keeps me employed and far away from the threat of ever having to step foot back into a 9 to 5 job. So, I hope you enjoy it and tell your friends. If nothing else, I'm sure they'll appreciate the insanity since it seems to be something that so many can relate to. Plus, unlike in the corporate world, you don't need a parachute for this activity.

Cheers.

For my father, Roy Hamlin, the greatest mentor a girl could ask for.

CHAPTER ONE

Everything I Ever Needed to Know I Learned in Kindergarten

The Commandments of Good Management

- I've probably forgotten more than you'll ever know.
- The lost-and-found just called and said they had found a spine. They were wondering whether it was yours.
- If you were on fire, I'd buy marshmallows and invite everyone else to eat.

While those three comments are humorous, it really is no laughing matter to be in a situation where you feel that way towards someone else. Being stuck in a lousy work environment can have several detrimental effects. It can lead to a variety of stress-related physical ailments, depression, anxiety, and work burn-out. These are all things that dampen a company's productivity and bottom line.

There are several things workers can do to alleviate work-stress: Reset your limits, spend your breaks differently, take vacations, or exercise. However, a lot depends on the type of management in place.

One day as I was doing some business research online, I came across "Everything I Ever Needed to Know I learned in Kindergarten" written by Robert Fulghum. It's a fundamental yet comprehensive list that really encompasses the important things. It relates to more than just kindergarten. I've read this list before (as I'm sure most of you have) and thought how appropriate it was for life. I found it to be a very insightful bit of wisdom.

Then when I thought more about it, I realized that it could easily be applied to basic management principles. So I decided to come up with the list you have in front of you: The Commandments of Good Management:

Don't take things that aren't yours. If your subordinate has a great idea, promote it; don't steal it! You'll be praised for fostering bright and motivated workers.

You stealing someone else's ideas does show (in some twisted way) that you value that person and their ideas, but you need to give credit where it's due. Stealing anything from others is wrong, but stealing ideas may put you at a bigger disadvantage in the future with your employees. In doing this, you will automatically lose their respect. Additionally, they'll probably be less likely to go out of their way to help you.

Warm cookies and cold milk are good for you. So is respect and positive reinforcement. Show respect where due and give positive reinforcement to foster a healthy team environment. People will thank you for it later. Developing good listening and communications skills will help earn you the respect from your subordinates as well as your coworkers. It shows them respect. Be sure that your words and deeds contribute to a healthy corporate culture.

Live a balanced life – learn some and think some and draw and paint and sing and dance and play and work every day some. There's more to life than work. Don't expect your staff to be at the office till all hours every day. They deserve down-time. Burnt-out employees bring down productivity. Do your best to motivate your employees. You'll be glad you did; they'll be eager to take on more responsibility and their enthusiasm will spread to others. Conversely, negativity will lead to high turnover and a general environment with diminished productivity. This is what hurts business; managers need to be aware of it.

Good managers possess the following skills: They understand people, they set reasonable boundaries, and are excellent communicators. They also allow others a certain amount of freedom to do their work and be creative.

Something that's important to remember is that good managers know that they don't manage people, they manage work. We cannot control others, just the situation. We can only control ourselves and our actions. That's not an opinion; that's a fact. Get used to it.

Share everything. Don't keep your people in the dark. The more they know, the more they can contribute (*Psssst! It's not about you. Even though you believe it is, it's not. Learn to trust a little*.) If you hired them, you should be able to trust them. C'mon, we're all adults here.

Play fair. Don't allocate a ridiculous amount of work and then derail them or set them up for failure. Although so many managers do this, either unwittingly or on purpose, it serves no purpose other than create friction. At the end of the day, do you really want to deal with those problems?

Additionally, don't ask your subordinates to do that which you yourself are not willing to do. That's a big pet peeve of mine. Nothing – well, almost nothing – makes a manager look more slimy than when they refuse to learn the jobs of their subordinates before moving up. You should know what their job is, know how to do it, and help out when they really need it.

Don't hit people. Can you say lawsuit?

Put things back where you found them. Or better yet, when talking about things like confidence and self-esteem, don't take those at all! Do what you can to build these things in the people that report to you; they'll respect you for it!

Of course, it's possible that you don't care about their respect. You might only care about what those from up top think, right? Well here's news for you: the peon of today could be tomorrow's vice president at the company. Don't you want that to be a favorable relationship?

Clean up your own mess. Don't expect others to correct your mistakes or take the heat for it; act your age and take responsibility. I mean, I've heard you preach volumes on things like accountability. Do you even know what that means? You get upset when someone makes a mistake but I have yet to hear you say, "Hmmm, was there a breakdown in communication on my part that might have lead to this?" You want to talk about accountability, let's start from the top. Everyone should be accountable. Funny though, how the bat-$#@%-crazy manager rarely is.

Say you're sorry when you hurt somebody. If you're wrong, admit it. Trying to cover up mistakes only leads to lying and looking like a big jerk. Don't let anyone else take the fall for it. Think of the Golden Rule: treat others the way you want to be treated. Of course, if you're "The Boss", you think you're untouchable. Granted, you answer to someone else and not to your support staff, but think about how you would want your boss to treat you if they're not already treating you like that.

Wash your hands before you eat. This is basic hygiene, folks. If you're sick, then take a sick day – no one wants your germs! Don't be a martyr. I can't tell you how many times I've seen this. Sick days are for staying home and resting. Of course, they could be for other things like running errands and going shoe shopping, but really, their primary purpose is to allow you rest when you truly need it. Use them. How many times have you seen, during the wintertime especially, an epidemic of flus and colds? Bad enough you give your staff grief on a daily basis, don't give them your sick germs too.

Flush. See "Clean up your own mess".

Take a nap every afternoon. If you can't allow an afternoon siesta, at least be sure that your people have the opportunity to walk away for lunch. They should not be expected to work through it. There comes a time when you just need to step away in order to gain a fresh perspective. Enforce this. We get it: deadlines come up and need to be met. It's crucial to conducting business. But keep a keen eye on your staff to ensure that no burnout occurs as a result of it. Stressed out employees are ripe for conflict. This is easily avoidable if you just allow them the time to walk away every so often.

When you go out in the world, watch out for traffic, hold hands and stick together. Don't throw your employees under the bus. Do for them and they'll do for you. At least give them the benefit of the doubt.

It is generally expected that subordinates will be protected by their supervisors. Good, bad or indifferent... part of the "team" mentality is that someone has your back. This is the way it ought to be – but just so rarely is.

Let me share with you a little story about a time a subordinate got thrown right under a bus by her bat-$#@%-crazy manager. This was an email I received from Mary:

> "It was a time when Miss Manager came back from an extended absence. She was out of the office for several months.
>
> During her time out, I reported directly to her boss, Miss Understand. Right around then, the department hired a contingent employee to help out on the team. Miss Understand called me into her office and told me

that Temp A was going to work on Project A... and be reporting to *my* idiot boss. It made sense to me since Project A was more related to my idiot boss' expertise. I sat directly across from her desk as she told me this. There was no mistaking what was said.

When Miss Manager came back to work, she and I had a conversation about Temp A. I indicated that Miss Understand said Temp A was to work on Project A. She said that she heard differently, but I insisted that it was Project A. We wrapped up our conversation and I went back into my office.

Not five minutes later I had a call from Miss Understand, who asked me to see her in their office. Okay.

I walked in there and Miss Manager closed the door behind me. Her boss asked where I got the notion that Temp A was to work on Project A.

"You told me so." I answered.

She shook her head vigorously, "I never told you that. I told you that Temp A was to work on Project B."

Oh really? Project B was MY JOB.

"If you told me that Temp A was to work on Project B, I'm sure that's something I would have remembered. That's not what you said." I said.

Her face turned bright red and a vein in her temple began to dance. "I NEVER said that to you."

So now I'm just shocked that she's raising her voice to me. Totally bewildered, I look to Miss Manager who is just glowering at me.

I asked her what was going on and she merely shrugged her shoulders. Thanks, you cold-hearted moron. I love the smell of tire rubber in the morning.

So I looked back at her boss and told her, "I sat directly across from you in this very chair here when you told me. I didn't misunderstand you."

I thought she was going to slam her fist into the desk. I started to feel warm from my toes all the way to my earlobes. "That's not what you heard because that's NOT what I said."

In order to hope for any kind of escape, I caved. "Okay, whatever you say. That's not what I walked out of here with... but fine... Temp A is to work on Project B. Fine. May I leave now?"

Then she let me leave. To this day I never understood why she got so upset with me over it. What was the big deal anyway? Even still... why would anyone need to get so nasty? It still baffles me. Whatever."

Be aware of wonder. Remember the little seed in the Styrofoam cup: the roots go down and the plant goes up and nobody really knows how or why, but we are all like that. Your people are only as good as you train them. Spend the time to mentor your staff and guide them along on their career. When they're superstars, they'll have you to thank. Unless they're too good for their benefit and pose a threat to you. Or at least in your mind they pose a threat. In which case you can bully them until they're either on the verge of a nervous breakdown or they quit because they can't take any more of you. Either way works for you because if they do stay they'll be so badly beaten that you'll have knocked their ingenuity right out of them.

Goldfish and hamsters and white mice and even the little seed in the Styrofoam cup - they all die. So do we. Like money, you can't take your knowledge and experience to the grave, so share it! Then again, if you have no knowledge in the first place it explains why you never share any. Can't pass along what ain't there, right? Certainly.

And then remember the Dick-and-Jane books and the first word you learned - the biggest word of all - LOOK. Appreciate and support the people that work for you. If they know you're there for them and see what you do for them, you will gain immeasurable results from them.

Threatening them also works. I've seen the mightiest of employees shrink to mere shells of the individuals they used to be after their managers got through with them. The work got done but not before the employees had to start taking antidepressants to deal with the pressure they were under. Naturally, these were hard working people from the get go, but look at what they can do now that they're medicated!

A good leader knows what it takes to succeed. Most of it is contained in this list of commandments. We need to remember the old saying, "You can lead a horse to water but you can't make him drink". Knowing the things that motivate people and implementing them is true success. If people are respected and given the freedom to do their jobs, managers will receive unending rewards from it. It's possible to glean enormous results with very little. We just need to know where to start.

We need to pay attention to life's little lessons. There's a reason why children attend kindergarten; it serves as a solid foundation for the rest of their lives. Luckily, we have the experience and wisdom to know that.

CHAPTER TWO

The Corporate Bloodsuckers Moved Your Cheese

"You do not lead by hitting people over the head – that's assault, not leadership." - *Dwight D. Eisenhower*

Who Moved My Cheese is a book that's supposed to be an endearing metaphor about mice that learn how to think "outside the box" and broaden their horizons in response to the changing times in their little world. I want to squash those mice. I've been a vegetarian for almost sixteen years and that's how I feel about those little guys. Cute, nothing.

They set the stage for disaster. Let me explain.

The point they make is obvious; in order to move forward in business you need to move with the times and be adaptable. This is the best way to be successful. Those who don't change and remain rigid in their ways and practices are stepped on, "starved out", or simply left behind.

In theory, this is good advice. I mean, how many of you have been told "No" to trying something new because, "It's always been done this way"? Well, to me the book came to mean something else.

When my boss handed this book to me a few years ago, I should have seen the writing on the wall. Boy, was I naïve. I interpreted the book to be what it was: a metaphor.

What I think my boss was really saying: "We're going to knock you on your ass with constant 'restructuring' and tell you how it's good for you. Meanwhile, we'll increase your workload, berate you, belittle you, and walk all over you. Basically, we're going to do everything we can to either push you out or just make you cry like a little girl with a skinned knee... because we feel like it."

This book was merely a sign of events to come. How I wish I'd had the foresight to know.

My Boss, the Tick

Bosses (particularly bad ones), can be likened to ticks for several reasons:

1: The first immature stage (larvae, which are many times called seed ticks) have only six legs. These larvae must find and attach themselves to a host in order to get a blood meal. After obtaining this blood meal they usually drop to the ground, shed their skin and emerge as 8-legged nymphs.

Bad managers are usually bad because they manage people. In order to cause any real damage they need to latch on to a poor unsuspecting schmuck for survival. Surprisingly, as incompetent as some bosses appear, they're the ones that usually get promoted... just like the tick. The big differing point here is that the boss remains in an immature state.

2: Adult ticks may require several days of feeding before they are able to reproduce. Male hard ticks usually die soon after mating, and females die soon after laying their eggs.

Idiot managers try again and again to spread their venom (unwittingly of course). After a while, their host wears down and gives in. Unfortunately, the managers don't die. They get moved to the corner office. Why won't they die???

3: Most ticks spend the bulk of their life on or near the ground, waiting for a suitable host animal. Since they cannot run, hop, fly or move quickly, ticks must climb onto an appropriate object such as tall grass or weeds or up onto fences and siding of buildings.

Most bat-$#@%-crazy bosses are like this too. They exist on the lowest rung of the morality ladder. They lack the intelligence and creativity to do things on their own which is why they have hosts, I mean, employees. The bright employees are the ones who usually do all the work without getting the credit. Then, after all of their hard work, the idiot bosses will further suck the life out of them by telling them they did a lousy job and steal away any shred of self-confidence they may still have about themselves.

4: Most ticks will feed on blood from a wide variety of animals, with only a few tick species feeding on but one kind of host.

Many bully bosses will continue to abuse one employee. Usually it's the employee with confidence, a great reputation, willingness to please and good relationships with others. You know, the ones that actually pose a threat to their boss (at least in the boss' mind). After a few too many "feedings", the employee begins to blame themselves for not being able to stand up straight after they've been completely sucked dry. They're even willing to have transfusions so the tick boss can continue feeding.

Suckers.

How to Beat the Office Bully

There's gotta be a better way to do this. Were you ever bullied as a child on the playground? At some time or another, we've all been the victim of a bully's tactics. When you're a kid it feels like the world is collapsing in on you when you're under attack. You usually feel pretty helpless. Let's face it; kids can be pretty mean.

So now we're all grown up, at least biologically. We go to work like good worker bees and we run into the same nonsense but on a "big people" level. This in no way means that the bully's antics are any more mature, mind you. It is this one aspect that makes being bullied in the workplace even more frustrating. Didn't we leave all this behind???

Insecurity can do some serious damage. And where there's insecure people, there's going to be conflict and struggle. What makes that even worse is when the conflict is between a manager and a subordinate.

In the book *Staying Sane,* Dr. Raj Persaud offers several suggestions to help meet/beat the office bully on solid ground. As I've said regarding others' suggestions on the topic, these are logically good ideas... but what people need to remember is that when dealing with a bully, you're not dealing with a logical person in a logical situation.

Let's take a look at some of these suggestions:

1. Get witnesses: never be in a place where the bully and yourself are alone together. Always speak to the bully in the presence of others.

Good idea, but you might be asking for more trouble if you refuse to meet with the bully (especially if the bully is your boss) for meetings or any other routine things that you would normally meet with them over. If the bully is a smart person, they'll find a way around this.

Take a look at Susie's story: "When I suggested to Inhuman Resources that they get involved in future meetings with my spazz of a boss, I got written up for insubordination. They sided with my boss and stated that I was being unreasonable -- regardless of my complaints or the fact that I could back it all up."

2. Warn the person who is causing the problem to stop. Explain - in front of witnesses - that you will take it further. Alternatively, you can get someone to do this on your behalf or write them a letter. Be firm and confident, but not aggressive or confrontational. Explain clearly the behavior you consider bullying and let them know exactly how they should behave.

*This might work -- or at least convey the message that you won't take any nonsense. But the key is to have witnesses. If you do this one-on-one, the bully may take it as a threat and escalate the situation. **It happened to me.***

3. If it fails to stop then you may decide to make a formal complaint. All companies should have a grievance procedure which you should follow to the letter. Again, advice from a union rep or sympathetic manager can be crucial.

This is always an option. Hopefully, if you take this route people will take you seriously and listen to your side of the story. However, they probably have to listen to the other side as well. If your company agrees with you, then you have more in your favor. If not, then be prepared to leave the company (if you haven't already started looking for another job) or be fired.

4. Adapt your response to the specific situation of the person bullying you - if it is a boss consider going further up the tree to their superiors.

*This is another good suggestion. I've heard success stories from individuals who have taken this path. If it is an option for you, then take it above your boss' head. There's a chance that they aren't aware of what's happening. **On the other hand:** They may not only know what's going on, they may also be the perpetrators behind the bully's deeds.*

Angie found herself in a spot that left her feeling utterly helpless: "I was in a situation once where I had a "Standoff" meeting between my bat-$%#@-crazy-manager and Inhuman Resources. His manager sat right beside him - for his support. Not only would his boss not speak to me, she refused to even make eye contact."

So, you have options for certain. They just might not all be good options. At the end of the day you need to decide what you're comfortable with and move forward with that. But try to remember that saying or doing something for yourself is always better than doing nothing. If nothing else, it will help you feel better (for standing up for yourself), and it will send a message (possibly) to others in your organization that something's going on.

The Con Game

Unmotivated workers sometimes lack the confidence to get the job done. This should hardly come as a surprise to anyone that's worked for anybody else. However, as a manager, it's up to you to determine if this is in fact holding your employee back.

In an article that I read by Thad Green, he says that "good managers learn to recognize when an employee says he can do something but doesn't mean it". One of the responses managers should look out for is (and this one gives me goose bumps), *"If everything works out well then I should be able to…"* in regards to getting a project done. According to Thad, this is a sure sign of a **confidence** issue.

I say that it's a sure sign that the manager could be a completely incompetent schmuck who doesn't know their ass from their elbow. Let me explain why.

The employee in question could be a perfectly able - and willing - individual. As a matter of fact, this person may have even been a high achiever on previous projects. So why the change? Perhaps the idiot boss has interfered one too many times preventing this employee from being able to get anything done, thus killing their confidence.

It's true; if you meddle in someone's work or throw something else in the mix that is completely unrelated but just as demanding and expect it to all be done at the same time, you're going to have problems. I assure you of this. So now all of a sudden this person that you're giving a project is answering you with, *"If everything works out well then I should be able to…"*. This means that they don't know what you're going to do to trip them up or sabotage them. They're not mind-readers.

If you do what a good manager is supposed to do, then you'll let them do their job and they'll produce results. **Get in their way and they won't**. It's that simple.

So then Thad goes on to say that the **three questions** a manager should ask an employee who exhibits these confidence issues are:

-Do you know what is expected? (*Yes, I'm not an idiot, thank you very much. I've only been in this job for YEARS*).

-Do you think what's expected is attainable? *(It won't be if you have anything to do with it)*.

-Can you do what is being asked of you and can you do it on time? *(Knowing you, you'll throw every obstacle you can think of plus nine other projects that need to be done concurrently and then you'll write me up for not getting this first project done, you dolt)*.

Here's some questions of my own that I think the employee should be asking in return:

- Did you get your degree out of a Cracker Jack box?
- Were you teased as a child?
- Have you been skipping doses on your meds?

I mean, honestly.

A Hard Act to Follow

My father used to tell me that bosses sometimes did ridiculous things because of their egos. My general feeling on that is it's OK to "act up" on occasion if the genius juices are flowing and the individual truly is great at what they do. Plus, as far as my experience goes, many of these people still keep an eye on their employees and take care of them. These are generally the people that preach – and live – the "work hard, play hard" credo.

However, to this day I have yet to bear witness to the rhyme and reason behind a manager's antics. I've seen lots of acting up, but little evidence of brains behind the act. Poor me, I know.

I worked in sales for several years. As I'm sure you're aware, different organizations take different approaches to selling their product or brand. One of the most interesting acts I caught along the way was one by a very bright (and well dressed) man who managed a group of account executives.

What I witnessed was no less than the most appalling display of ego imaginable. What's even more amazing is that I was present, as was everyone else from the office, in a weekly sales meeting where the manager proceeded to pick on an account executive. He picked and picked so brutally that it was embarrassing for me to sit and watch. I know others were uncomfortable; however, less sensitive to it since they had been exposed to this person's behavior for some time. What's more appalling is the fact that this was the everyday fare. While I didn't witness it on this occasion, the victim of the abuse eventually broke down and cried. Not only that, it wasn't uncommon to see tears shed in the midst of the meeting.

I'm certainly not suggesting that this kind of behavior is acceptable, but really, if you need to admonish a subordinate – or anyone – please be sure to do so behind closed doors with only the applicable party present. Nobody needs to witness that, let alone deserves being on the receiving end of that.

The Dilbert Principle

I read Scott Adams' *The Dilbert Principle*. What a unique book. This guy really tells it as it is. What I find so interesting is that he really tells it as it is and spares no details. I've operated cloak-and-dagger for such a long time it's odd to know that I don't have to continue looking over my shoulder every five minutes.

Let me tell you about my life since my departure from corporate America (a.k.a. The Prison Break). There is no more clarity now than there was then, I can tell you that. In a way, those miserable events leading up to my exodus feel like they occurred a lifetime ago and to another person. Although I wouldn't go as far to say that I've developed Post Traumatic Stress Syndrome (like many in my situation have), it has been years since I have not been so closely scrutinized. My shoulders are just starting to go back to their "resting" position, which is relaxed and away from my ears.

Have you ever experienced a surreal event or witnessed the destruction of something that you might have thought indestructible? Say, for instance Whitney Houston's fall from grace (who would have seen that coming fifteen years ago?) or take even Steve Irwin's tragic death (we wouldn't have been as surprised if it was a crocodile!). These were very real events that had unreal aspects to it. My job experiences were just like that; very real events with some completely unreal – and sad - twists and turns.

I'm almost too happy to oblige and stay out of it, but I won't keep my mouth shut. One of my new goals is to completely break the habit of looking over my shoulder. Hence, this book.

What's the point?

It happens too often that a manager will throw a subordinate under the proverbial bus. Or, if there is praise to be had they'll steal it and do what they need to in order to make you look bad. Insecurity is the key ingredient in today's dish of the day. It's unfortunate that insecure individuals really seem to be at the core of so much of this nonsense. The good news is, you'll know very quickly if your boss falls into this category. A good manager will praise you appropriately and give constructive criticism when warranted. If you have a bad manager, you'll already be able to smell the burnt rubber.

Lesson learned:

Who stole the handbook that taught managers how to be managers? Clearly, these managers (in these stories at least) need some direction.

1-Work is about getting the job done. Getting in the way of

that holds up the process and sets the standard for failure. In addition, it puts more pressure on you, John Q Workerbee, to perform. So, in the beginning you may have been on target, but with interference it set you back; even though your idiot boss still expects things by the original deadline.

What you can do:
Ask them to specify which is priority. If they will not commit to doing this then you need to let them know that at the current rate of activity and with any further "interference" (and of course you put that as nicely as possible), you need to negotiate a new deadline.

This is key: *If your manager is going to alter the original project, they need to allow for these changes. If they tack more work on and toss newer, unrelated projects on your desk that need to be done first, they have to allow time for the original project to get done. It's that simple. Do not fall for the "You-should-be-able-to-figure-this-out-for-yourself-and-do-whatever-you-need-to-in-order-to-get-it-done" routine. This will only cause damage to your self esteem; it is not within your power to alter the definitions of time and space as these people want you to believe.*

2-Wouldn't you rather have a fan club than a fight club?

Creating tension will only cause problems; they will not lead to work getting done faster or more efficiently. Be a part of the solution, not the problem. Create a fighting force that will accomplish amazing feats and make you look like a superstar. No one will do that for you if you put them down or threaten them.

3-Bullies are for the school yard... the elementary school yard. They have no place in business.

As later chapters in this book will tell you, working with bullies is extremely difficult. At the end of the day, they don't want to work with you – or anyone. Unless your company can help tame this person or eliminate them, you're either on your own with your career in potential sabotage, or you're out the door (whether from being fired by this incompetent snake or from you quitting).

I mean, at the end of the day if you've done your job right, there would be no need for the boss to be anything other than grateful to you for doing what you're supposed to, right?

I get it: what do we expect when we accomplish that which we're hired to do, right? This isn't about anyone bowing down to us. This is about courtesy and mutual respect (and of course, positive reinforcement). We do not expect you to lick our boots, but you *can* repay us not just by giving us a paycheck every week, but by not finding fault with something completely unrelated and solely for the sake of putting us down. There's always tomorrow to nitpick about an issue that needs attention. Right now we need to feel like we're not total failures. We'd appreciate it if you can remember that from time to time.

CHAPTER THREE

Hand Holding for Dummies

"I don't know anything about music. In my line you don't have to." - *Elvis Presley*

If YOU Were the Perpetrator

There's been plenty said on bullying in the workplace. Heaven knows I sure have my piece to say about it. I've even seen books out there *for* idiot bosses (*How to Work for an Idiot* by John Hoover is a gem). As a matter of fact, I recently saw an article on careerbuilder.com about the perpetrators of workplace bullying.

The thing is, no one is going to read an article or a book and have an "a-ha!" moment of "I'M THE IDIOT!!!" Really, if it were that simple, more people would be paying attention to start with and there wouldn't be ugly managers in charge of people. At best, they'd be left alone with angry ant farms to control.

So let's just face up to the nasty reality that idiot bosses will very likely NOT change any time soon. If others in the company notice an idiot's behavior and have the ability to effect change, then fantastic – my hat's off to you. However, most of us live in the real world, most of the time anyway.

Inhuman Resources is there to protect the company's hide and incompetent managers are left in place: it's the victimized employees who are left to suffer more abuse, damaged reputations, and diminished self-esteems. They will have to fly the coop to be rid of a bully boss. Unless of course one of those

Acme anvils happens to come crashing down on them like in the Roadrunner cartoons.

That would be so cool.

A Vicious Cycle

Some people say the way to appease a micromanager is to keep them informed of all goings-on at all times. Let me be the first to tell you that this doesn't have a high success rate.

The following is John's story:

"I copied my boss on all email correspondences. I did this in an effort to keep her informed. You know what happened then? Two minutes after I sent an email out (any email for that matter, and of course I sent dozens of emails a day), she'd call and say, "Well what you should have said was this..." OR "you should have said it this way", OR "I would have said..."

So then I got caught in a cycle of telling her what I was going to send and then sent it to her first so that she could "proof" it (or format the hell out of it, put bullet points in it, bold/color the font, call out the band for a parade, etc).

That STILL did not guarantee that she wouldn't call later with "suggestions". As a matter of fact, it gave her an opportunity to judge me further, pick my *correct* work apart and trample all over my self-esteem.

Then on the rare occasion that I answered an email and didn't copy her - like for a ridiculous question that didn't warrant cc'ing the whole planet - she always had a way of finding out and ripping me a new one about it."

The moral to this story is - you cannot cure a micromanager, nor can you appease them. Telling them everything that you do only starts a vicious cycle.

So stop the insanity and back away from the email! They need to get over themselves and grab some self-esteem... THEIR OWN!!!

What Makes a Bully?

At various times I've used names to describe idiot bosses, toxic managers and other sociopaths that we call our supervisors.

Now, with some help from Sam Horn's book *Taking the Bully by the Horns*, I'd like to take a brief look at why they are the way they are. Ultimately though, I don't really care. It's not my problem that these people are bullies and it's certainly not my burden. But, it's interesting information nonetheless and I'm going to share it with you.

So What Makes a Bully?

Lack of Self-Confidence: Confident people feel good about who they are and how they live their lives. Bullies lack confidence so they therefore gang up on those of us that don't in order to make themselves feel better.

Does your boss find fault with everything that you do? Under the strongest microscope, it is inevitable that you will find some fault with everyone. These individuals exist to do just that and then exploit it.

For example, I had an idiot manager who would look through a five hundred page report that I submitted and then complain that I didn't bold the font - on one word - on one of the page's headers, but I did on the other four hundred and ninety-nine. She'd then use that to say that I lacked attention to detail.

I have another example that I can't fail to use: grammatical corrections. This manager found some minute fault with every email or memo possible. Even after I explained that I was a published writer, I still had my writing red-lined in a very grade-school-English-teacher kind of way. That was always delightful.

They Don't Care: People who bully do not possess a sense of empathy or guilt. They either don't think they're bullying, don't care or they simply enjoy doing it.

I asked my bat-$#@%-crazy manager to cease-and-desist when she used to do this to me, but she never did. Even worse, she had the backing of her management to continue demeaning and belittling me.

No Negative Consequences: If no one's going to stop them, the bullying will continue.

In my case, I took the proper route and documented everything and addressed it with Inhuman Resources. *What happened*: I was placed on written warning. Then HR told me that my manager was allowed to say whatever she wanted about me in my annual reviews and they would stand behind her - without even listening to my side of the story.

Bullies are Arrogant: I never gave my boss enough credit for this... but, since in the previous point there were no negative consequences, she continued to beat me down and use me as a welcome mat.

They Have a Certifiable Psychological or Biological Problem: I'm just not even going to go here... you're probably bright enough to know what this could mean.

<u>What's the point?</u>

Managers need a clue. Just because your boss got to where they are does not mean they magically know how to manage anything other than their own workload (and my experience shows that at least one couldn't manage so much as an ant farm or a newspaper route). As mentioned in Chapter One, there's a lot that goes into working well with others and heading up a successful team.

Managers don't always have common sense. There isn't too much I can say about this one; your boss either has the smarts or doesn't. If they do, then you might have something to work with… if they don't, then there isn't anything you can do about that. You need to decide if this is something that you can learn to live with or transfer to a different department or find a new job altogether. Thanks for playing.

Lesson learned:

Managers do not want a clue. It's nice that you have a degree from a good college and maybe someone's good reference, but in their little realm only they exist. They are in denial and do not believe that we could possibly be talking about them. THEY WILL NEVER ADMIT IT SO DON'T TRY. You want to change something? Try a new dinner recipe or buy new underwear. These are the kinds of things you can change. Forget about your boss and just keep collecting that paycheck.

CHAPTER FOUR

Run It Up a Flagpole and See If Anyone Salutes It

"Some cause happiness wherever they go; others, whenever they go." - *Oscar Wilde*

What Flavor of Crazy is Your Boss?

The Physicist Manager: Manages you on a cellular level.

The CSI Manager: Manages your DNA.

The Construction Manager: Always throws roadblocks in your path.

The Tazmanian Devil Manager: Whips through the office like a tornado and un-does all your hard work in seconds.

The Sociopath Manager: Changes their mind constantly on submitted projects and denies it. However, they scream at you and belittle you anyway for the hell of it.

The Narcissistic Manager: Demands the red-carpet treatment while getting the morning coffee.

The Martyr Manager: Works twenty-two out of twenty-four hours a day... how come you don't?

The Jell-O Manager: Spineless.

The Frustrated School Teacher Manager: Tells you where to put your commas.

The Robot Manager: Since it isn't human, it has no feelings and shows no emotions.

The Blamethrower Manager: It's always your fault... regardless of whether you can prove otherwise.

The Venus Fly Trap Manager: Interesting to look at, but will swallow you whole if you get too close.

Attila the Manager: Will storm in and beat you to the ground and expect you to genuflect.

The Third Reich Manager: Annihilates all employees who report to him.

A Coursebook in Mis-Management:

I've read that workplace bullies are often highly intelligent people. It's funny for me to think of the moron managers I've known as smart when they exhibited so many traits to the contrary. However, it got me to thinking: Just where exactly do these people receive their education?

Then I did a little research and found it: A course book in Mis-Management (at an institution that shall remain nameless). In order to receive a degree in this major, credits are required in the following areas:

Egotism 101

School Yard Domination (first and second year students only)

Ballroom Bullying

Power Trips 101

Mastery of Illusion (works especially well with Power Trips 101)

World Dictators (emphasis on modern leaders: Mussolini, Stalin, Hitler, Pol Pot, Castro, etc)

Dictatorship (this class is for seniors only. Must successfully complete World Dictators to be eligible for enrollment in this class)

Delusions of Grandeur

Brow Beating (available to students at every level)

Micromanagement (in order to be considered for acceptance into this class, a written paper is required on the topic: 101 Ways to Undermine Your Staff)

De-Motivation (training is geared toward those individuals bent on thwarting any bright and ambitious worker that will report to them in the future).

The bat-$#@%-crazy managers I know must have graduated with (dis)honors from this program!

It Has a Name: Workplace Bullying

I came across an interesting website at www.bullyonline. org that talks about bullies at work and goes further into detail about what bullying is, who is targeted, why it happens, etc.

Although it's encouraging that there exists a fair amount of information on the topic, it sucked when it happened to me. I used to love my job. No joke, it all changed in one day.

The site's bullying list is very long so I'll summarize some points most relevant to me with my notes in *italics*:

People who are bullied find that they are:

1: Constantly criticized and subjected to destructive criticism (often euphemistically called constructive criticism, which is an oxymoron) - explanations and proof of achievement are ridiculed, overruled, dismissed or ignored.

Once, in an effort to push for a promotion, I developed enhancements to a report that I produced. This enhancement made it possible to finish the report faster and in a more streamlined manner. It didn't rival the invention of the wheel, but it was an enhancement to make the report flow smoother and save valuable time.

To say that it was shot down is an understatement. Miss Manager may as well have blown her nose with the report. Long story short, I didn't get the promotion, and when all was said and done it reared its ugly head in my annual review a few months later. When my supervisor brought up my contributions, she said only that "there may have been one or two" but that they were "of no consequence". Thank you for stomping all over my intelligence and self-confidence.

In the end, I was moved into a different job and my report enhancement never came to fruition. However, my old job was then split up and given to a team of four people. So, I'm guessing that they had the time to do the report the long way. More power to 'em.

2: Forever subject to nit-picking and trivial fault-finding (the triviality is the giveaway).

This fits many bat-$#@%-crazy managers like a glove. Of course, I can't leave out the grammatical corrections ("this comma belongs here instead of here" and "this word needs to be bold and in blue Arial font" – or any variation thereof. How about I shove that comma down your throat in an active grenade?)?

3: Undermined, especially in front of others; false concerns are raised, or doubts are expressed over a person's performance or standard of work - however, the doubts

lack substantive and quantifiable evidence, for they are only the bully's unreliable opinion and are for control, not performance enhancement.

My oh my, this just keeps getting better. I'm beginning to wonder if the term "work-place bullying" was coined just for me.

I've been harangued me on this very point in my annual review and in my daily performance. Yet I received no examples. I wonder why?

4: Isolated and excluded from what's happening (this makes people more vulnerable and easier to control and subjugate).

I'm sure Steven's story is not uncommon:

"A long time ago, a temp was brought in to lend a hand on my team, though not under my supervision (I was already a departmental pariah by then).

One day, I watched as this temp walked into Miss Manager's office followed behind her boss, Miss Treatment. Since the office was next to mine and they left the door open, I could hear what they were discussing: work directly related to my job. So all the alarms in my head went off and I got up and stood in her doorway.

Miss Treatment gave me her back and did not once attempt to look at me. Am I really that intimidating? Or was the scenery out the window more interesting? We'll never really know.

I asked if there was a meeting that they forgot to tell me about.

She looked caught in the act as she answered, "No". The atmosphere in the room shifted with me standing there. She then proceeded to tell me that they were discussing something completely different. So she basically lied –right to my face. Either they thought I was too stupid to realize it or they just didn't care. That's a nice touch, I thought."

5: Set unrealistic goals and deadlines which are unachievable or which are changed without notice or reason or whenever they get near achieving them.

Someone must have spied on me... this list is REALLY accurate!!!

6: Subject to excessive monitoring, supervision, micro-management, recording, snooping etc.

Did I also mention that I was required to submit a daily status report... for a year?

Targets of bullying usually have these qualities:

Popularity (this stimulates jealousy in the less-than-popular bully):

I would say this applied to me... some even thought that I was my boss' supervisor.

Competence (this stimulates envy in the less-than-competent bully):

Just because they brag about working weekends does not make them more competent. Long hours are not indicative of being good at what you do; it just means that you have a lot of work to do.

I have and appreciate the ability to work smarter. To those that do not work smart: might I suggest a new strategy? Use your head -- it's that lump about three feet above your ass.

Intelligence and intellect:

Intelligence, me... intellect, me... That's two for me and NONE for you!

A sense of humor, including displays of quick-wittedness:

A butter knife is usually sharper than an idiot boss.

Ability to master new skills:

It's called the English language – learn how to use it! Take a public speaking class or something because when it comes to clarifying a point, simply repeating the same thing over and over explains nothing and people do NOT understand you! It's like shouting at a deaf person – they won't hear you and frankly, it's embarrassing to witness.

Helpful, always willing to share knowledge and experience:

Oh boy, was I head and shoulders above on this one.

You know, I'd like to say that I could go on and on but then I'd have nothing left to publish. But that would be wrong. I could go on and on and still have tales to tell from here ad infinitum.

When I told people that I was writing this book, they came out of the woodwork, wanting to tell their stories. These stories are the basis for this book.

Researcher Says Bullied Workers Need Outlet for Workplace Grievances

Cheers to another genius.

I have the perfect solution: the back of my hand meeting the side of my bat-$#@%-crazy manager's head. Repeatedly.

This does not mean in any way that I condone workplace violence. That would just create a nasty cycle. It's unnecessary and it's illegal.

I use the hand-smack as an example of a solution that would work for many people. It would work for people because there just aren't many other good solutions in place for the benefit of bullied workers. Inhuman Resources does not seem to be there for the employees (in many cases anyhow).

Let's see what other options there are... aside from filing a formal grievance with HR (which as I mentioned isn't likely to go over well), there aren't many choices that will alleviate a toxic situation for the employee. There's always the option to hire a lawyer and sue, although most people probably won't do that.

Then there's quitting the job, which seems to offer the best solution. It's the best solution because the bully boss will not likely change anytime in the foreseeable future. Also, it takes the bullied worker out of the dangerous environment. So now the stress-related health issues that developed during the last job can now be healed.

Those Who Can Do, Those Who Can't Bully

The following is taken from www.bullyonline.org It briefly details the difference between a **Good** manager (yay!) and a **Bully** (boo!). Hopefully you're more familiar with the first list than with the second.

A Good Manager:
- Leader
- Decisive
- Accepts responsibility
- Fair, treats all equally
- Respectful and considerate
- Leads by example
- Confident
- Good interpersonal skills
- Motivates
- Builds team spirit
- Uses influencing skills
- Cares about staff, the business, etc.
- Listens, guides, instructs
- Has high expectations (that staff will do well)
- Shares fairly
- Shares information freely
- Focused on the future

- Respected

The Bully:
- Coward
- Random, impulsive
- Abdicates responsibility
- Inconsistent, always critical, singles people out,
  shows favoritism
- Disrespectful and inconsiderate
- Dominates, sets a poor example
- Insecure, arrogant
- Poor interpersonal skills
- De-motivates
- Divisive, uses manipulation and threat
- Alienates, divides, creates fear and uncertainty
- Cares only about self
- Tells
- Has low expectations of everybody
- Controls and subjugates
- Withholds information, releases selectively, uses information
  as a weapon
- Obsessed with the past
- Loathed

Does Workaholic = Micromanager?

As you folks know, I have extensive experience working for micromanagers. While I do not believe that every workaholic is a micromanager, I would have to say this is the case most of the time. I'll tell you why.

Definition of a Workaholic: *One who has a compulsive and unrelenting need to work. It is sometimes linked to obsessive-compulsive disorder… just like someone who micromanages.*

Definition of a Micromanager: *One who directs or controls in a* *detailed, often meddlesome manner.*

As I've mentioned before, many micromanagers are individuals suffering from a compulsive disorder (which may be helped by a swift kick, or not).

Workaholic Behavior:
-Need to control
-Inflexibility
-Perfectionism
-You bring work home
-You think about work and how to "fix" things while at home
  or on vacation
-You want to do it all yourself; you do not properly delegate
  tasks

Micromanaging Behavior:
-Need to control
-Inflexibility
-Perfectionism
-Excessive criticism
-You want to do it all yourself; you do not properly delegate
  tasks

As with micromanagers, workaholics also tend to suffer from low self esteem. Micromanagement and workaholism are irrational behaviors. Both result in damaged/diminished social relationships, health problems and distorted thinking. Long ago, the term workaholic was used as a compliment. Since business changed and office cultures evolved, so has the term.

If someone you know is a workaholic, it may be time to throw them a life preserver and tow them to safety. They can be shown the way. If someone you know is a micromanager, tie an anvil to their ankle and throw them overboard. They won't be missed.

Manage Your Manager?

I've read several articles and books where individuals give tips on how to manage your manager. I found this idea interesting. Wrong, but interesting.

Rule #1 in "Good" Management: *You do NOT manage other people; you manage the work.*

This is what I think when I read these "tips" on managing your manager: *It sucks that managers try to control their subordinates but hey, it's okay for you to stoop to their level and control back.* What? Are we in grade school here?

I have three words for you folks: **Listen. Relax. Think.**

Listen to what your manager is actually saying to you. They're going nuts because they have a deadline to meet, right? Okay... so it's not about you. Get over that. **Relax.** If you've worked with this individual long enough you know the shots they're going to call. If you don't yet know what those shots are, then pay attention and find out what they will be; perhaps you can head them off at the pass the next go-around. **Think.** If you know how they operate and what they need, then be one step ahead of them and give them what they want! Then later on you can pat yourself on the back for being a hero.

Of course, this is provided your manager isn't out to sabotage your career. There are ways to get around your manager's incompetence or negligence:

First: Put in writing any project or request you are asked to do.

Second: Follow up on progress (1: So they don't freak out and/ or 2: So it gives them a clue as to what is going on).

Third: Deliver what you promise!

This is you managing *your* work. You cannot control other people. This advice is the same for employees and managers. You can only be responsible for how you react in certain situations. So be in control of that!

Your Knee-Jerk Reaction Might Be Kicking You

I read this article on Careerbuilder.com called "When You Love Your Job but Hate Your Boss". In it, the author says that a recent Gallup poll of one million workers revealed that the most common reason employees leave a company relates to a stressful or problematic relationship with their immediate supervisors. No real surprise there, right?

(On a sidebar, most supervisors believe that employees leave because they don't see themselves as adequately paid for their positions... not because it has anything to do with them... COME ON, FOLKS!)

So anyway, this article goes on to say that many people that leave their job due to this type of situation end up *regretting* their decision. Further into the article it details the things to do if you don't want to leave your job.

In my opinion, the most important thing to do is take a step back and really look at your situation. What's really going on at the office? Everyone has rough times at work. There's always times where you and the boss clash, or a problem comes up with a project, or a coworker or whatever, who knows. For the most part, people know when the job is no longer redeemable. And frankly, I can't think of so much as one person who regretted leaving their job because of a bad boss. Every person I know that left for that reason (and sadly, that's a lot of people) is much better off in their new job.

The article needs to stress that it's the *knee-jerk reaction* to quit the job that you should avoid. It would be silly to up and quit your job over one disagreement. If it's possible, try other routes around the boss. Show how good you are to the boss's boss and the company. This could help you. It may not, but if you like the job, you owe it to yourself to give it that shot.

Don't do what Kevin James' character (Albert Brenaman) did in the movie *Hitch* to score points with a woman. For those of you who didn't see it, he quit abruptly during a board meeting when his boss argued with him to stay in line (all to get a woman's attention). Funny movie, but don't do that in real life. Remember that your actions have consequences in the real world.

What's the point?

If you're lucky, your boss may exhibit a whole bunch of crazy packaged up in one body. There are just so many different kinds of incompetency. I could probably write a book just on that topic. If I did that though, I wouldn't get to share all of the fun stories I have now. It was a tough choice, but I think it'll be okay.

Lesson learned:

You're not alone out there... there's all kinds of messed up bosses. You may or may not be able to handle working with them all. Chances are you may not even be able to please them... ever. You know, someone once recommended that I go to my manager's boss on an issue that needed resolution. In some cases, your manager's boss may have no clue what they're doing. By you bringing them in the loop on something, it may make them sit up and listen. Of course, this only works if that person is a human being. For me it backfired, so I'm not sure that I'd recommend it. Of course, that's a choice you need to make. If it works, splendid. If it doesn't, I'd keep those resumes going out on a regular basis because there's little chance of you moving up once your boss finds out what you've done.

Take the chance or don't. I took the chance: I felt I had little choice. There just wasn't enough going for me yet on the job frontier for me to hand my notice in.

CHAPTER FIVE

English As a First Language

"Excuse me, I have to go to the ladies room. Actually, I need to make a telephone call, I was just too embarrassed to say."
– *Dorothy Parker*

What Are You Trying To Say?

One of the biggest reasons managers fail is because they're **lousy communicators**. These people will never rise to the level of a true leader.

Good leaders are individuals who know how to communicate. They are able to work with their employees to drive results. Part of what makes them a leader is the ability to **listen**. A manager that listens will hear the "true" meaning behind comments and adapt to them appropriately. Just as subordinates need to know what kinds of managers they have in order to provide them with what they need, leaders need to do this for their employees. If the employees have what they need, whether that's the necessary tools to do their job, motivation, or whatever, they will want to do that much more if they feel valued.

So stop and ask yourself if your message is conveyed clearly to your staff. *Is what you're saying the same as what your people are hearing?* Are you listening to them? Step beyond the boundaries of your office walls and actually interact with your team. Be open to their ideas and suggestions.

In addition to communicating with your team, know how to communicate with other departments. Listen to them too. Succeeding in business is all about forging alliances. However, in order to do this, you need to know how to talk to people!

Several years ago I was caught in a meeting where my manager could have benefited from having better communication skills. In an effort to settle a discrepant report, my supervisor called a meeting with an associate from sales and myself. As I witnessed the back-and-forth, my manager continued to seek the answer she wanted. It was important for us to get what we needed so we could move forward. It wouldn't have been so bad except that it didn't end there.

After she didn't get the answer she wanted (it was because there was no answer, not because the associate was not forthcoming with one), she proceeded to use the same (long-winded) explanation and ask the same (long-winded) question.

When she started to do it again for the third time, the sales associate became exasperated and walked out shortly after. My manager shook her head and said something about how uncooperative she was. Of course, if she was equipped with better communication skills, she might have been able to sweet talk her into some form of compliance, rather than hammer out the same demand.

When I spoke with this associate later, she only shook her head and asked how I was able to work with my boss every day. I replied that I was only able to do it because I had one foot out the door looking for other jobs.

My point is this: communicate, folks. If you're in a management position and you deal with people you're going to need this skill, I assure you. Not only that, it may help to also develop some type of sales skills or persuasive language skills. They both teach you how to interact with other human beings.

The Importance of Eye Contact

This simple, yet personalized, greeting or salute makes people feel important. Eye contact is extremely important for meaningful communication. Always remember; treat people the way you want to be treated.

I've seen firsthand the results when a manager refuses eye contact with their subordinates; it gets people talking and starts the gossip. Why? Maintaining eye contact helps to build trust and confidence with those you come into contact with. When that doesn't happen, people notice. Not only that, they begin to think (whether they're right or not) that something is wrong with the person.

If you notice too, it's not that natural. I'm not talking about being distracted by something, like working on your computer. While it is rude, it's not the same as sitting across from someone as they do nothing but stare at their desk – at nothing – while you're giving them an update on a project. It's a little weird.

So people begin to think things about this person. Their actions and motives become suspect. If establishing eye contact builds trust, then avoiding eye contact becomes suspicious. What are you trying to hide?

Who knows, maybe deep down they realize they're an idiot manager and just don't know how to pull themselves back up. It's never too late to brush yourself off and try again. What I find interesting is that people like this get to move up in the world. Just how exactly does this happen?

You know, researchers also say that people that have trouble making eye contact also have problems making friends. Of course they do. What kind of person would want to be friends with someone who can't even look them in the eye? It's just not inviting.

Say "Thank You"

"Who raised you?" is a question I always wanted to ask my managers. After so many years in corporate America I got tired of people being mean. There's just no need for it.

I live in the New York City area. Recently, I met two very nice ladies from Seattle, Washington. They commented on the number of friendly New Yorkers they encountered. This struck them as a little odd. It's a misconception that New Yorkers are nasty. We smile, we joke, and we help tourists on the subways. That's how we roll.

This is not the case in business. Once upon a time I had a nice career. Toward the end of my tenure things changed. The atmosphere went from kind and nurturing to back stabbing and nail biting (back stabbing on their part, nail biting on my part).

One of the factors that contributed to this feeling was one of antipathy from the upper powers-that-be. If I was expected to perform certain tasks and I did them, it would have been nice every so often to get a "Thank you". Or if I developed a new system of doing things or a new report to track data. None of these were taken seriously. If anything it was, "mmm hmmm, that's nice". No fanfare is necessary; just a small acknowledgment every so often that you like the job that I'm doing. As a matter of fact, I think that's called positive reinforcement.

I know I'm not alone in that. There are workers everywhere that feel unappreciated. Now let me tell you how much information is out there about motivation in the workplace. There are *gazillions* of books on the topic of how to jump-start the team and get them onboard to work that much harder. Here's a free tip: **SAY THANK YOU**. It won't cost the manager or the company anything to say this to their employees – particularly when warranted. If you want the behavior to continue, you have to reinforce it. How hard is that?

Didn't your mother tell you to say "Thank you" when someone did something nice for you like help you on a project that made you look like a superstar? Or help you to sort files so you didn't have to be in the office by yourself till ten o'clock at night?

Make Mom proud. Just say "Thanks" to the people that help you do your job.

It's Not Me, It's YOU

Nowadays the allure of being connected to email is extremely apparent. Perhaps this is why so many managers feel the need to be perfectionists when it comes to sending out memos. Even though there are devices like Blackberrys that make sending emails so easy and fast, there are those individuals that are true sticklers for the good old-fashioned memo. Personally, I think this attention it's an extension of pure micromanaging behavior.

A tale from "the front" as told to me by Jennifer:

"I have been working in my industry for a long time now. Some words used to describe my status are "Veteran", "Industry Expert", "Femme Fatale", etc. Okay, so mostly "Veteran" and "Industry Expert". The point I'm trying to make is that I know my business and I know what I'm talking about.

My boss needs to have a hand in EVERYthing that I do. Personally, the reason I think he gets ticked most often at me is because I don't share the details of when I go to the restroom during the course of the day. After all, it's probably the only thing I do that he can't control.

That said... as part of my job I am deeply immersed in emails. I know many people are. But on a daily basis, I receive an average of two hundred emails. Naturally, I have to respond to many of these.

If I need to address the masses in one email, I usually do it with one "grandaddy" of a memo. Since I'm working with my bat-S&$*# crazy manager for a few years now, I know that he likes the emails to be well-formatted pieces of art. Key words are highlighted and bullet-points go hand-in-hand with each new paragraph. On a good day, there may even be some color added on the font to really drive the point home of "Please be aware we are distributing these ridiculously large reports that you will probably never read".

As a rule, my manager requires all emails to pass through him to receive the stamp of approval before I'm allowed to send anything out. As I mentioned I am an industry veteran, an expert in my field. And yes, I am an adult. Believe me when I tell you, I have to bring my emails to my boss for him to proofread before I send them out. I am back in the fourth grade. Only I don't recall that experience as being so demeaning.

Let me tell you, I went to Catholic school where they enjoyed pounding the fear of God and the whole guilt "thing" into you. That was WAY better than treading the path to my idiot manager's office to have a simple memo approved.

I should also mention; these memos that I send out are more or less reconstituted notes from the recent and not-so-recent past. Since I know that my manager will find no less than five things wrong with a three-sentence paragraph, I decided to conduct a little experiment. I dug through my archived files to find emails that my manager sent out with the same or similar messages. I updated the emails to make them relevant and then passed them along for review.

Well wouldn't you know it: My bat-S&$*# crazy boss found no less than five things wrong with his own damn emails!"

The moral to today's story is: No matter how good you are at your job, there is no antidote for bat-S&$*# crazy managers. You may work for what resembles a human being, but they aren't. So take a deep breath and repeat as a mantra the words of Stuart Smalley, "I'm good enough, I'm smart enough, and gosh-darnit, people like me!" Then club your idiot boss like a baby seal, stuff him into trash bags and toss him into the incinerator.

Have a nice day!

When I Grow Up...

... I Wanna Be a Micromanager!

Let me see if I have what it takes to be a good micromanager:

As a person:

-*I have little-to-no confidence in myself and my abilities.* I'm miserable with who I am and the life I lead, and don't you dare tell me I need to "improve" myself.

-*I am an introvert.* I'm not the life of the party, people call me a wallflower.

-*Management is a people skill - it's not the job for someone who doesn't enjoy people.* Actually, I think I should be placed in charge of others so I can belittle them to make myself feel better about my shortcomings.

-*I am not always honest or straightforward.* It depends on what my manager tells me to say. I don't care if others trust me or not.

-*I am an EXcluder not an INcluder.* No one needs to know what I'm up to unless I say so. If I need anyone to do a project, I will withhold crucial information needed to complete the job. Let the suckers figure it out for themselves. They're here for my amusement anyway, no?

-*Managers must lead.* I tell my staff exactly where to go and I check up on them every ten minutes. "Status reports" are not unfamiliar words in my vocabulary. Time spent in the bathroom must be included on these.

On the job:

-I am consistently rigid, though my staff can depend on me changing my mind. I make all decisions, don't even bother telling me what you think, I don't care.

-I am a little bit crazy, what some people might call compulsive.

If I try new things at all and they fail, I blame the error on anyone that I can... even if they've left the company over a year ago.

-I make plans and schedules and work toward them. As for my staff, I will raise obstacles at every turn so that they cannot achieve their goals. Then, come review time, I'll badger them for it and justify why they shouldn't receive a raise.

-I view information as a tool to be used as I see fit. I will decide if I need to let my "team" in on anything.

Wow... I think the only challenge left for myself in a management role is to see how many bright, ambitious and talented individuals I can derail and tread on. Luckily for me, there are many companies that will not only hire me, but promote me into roles where I will manage teams of people.

They don't know how lucky they are.

Shades of Grey - Micromanagement Hell

DISGRNTLD76: why do I even get out of bed?

2GR8T4wrk: what happiness was she spreading today?

DISGRNTLD76: She sent me 3 emails to confirm that Worker Bee A called out sick.

2GR8T4wrk: ok

DISGRNTLD76: then she emails me a 4th time with this huge paragraph about the workers' hours and how she needs to know when they're working, when they're late or making up time. Then she ended by saying to call with any questions. So I did. And asked her - Is there a problem???

DISGRNTLD76: then she called me into her office

DISGRNTLD76: Yadda yadda, she's on me about keeping her in the loop when I have an employee out. I told her that I always let her know. Then she makes a face and says, "Not always." Oh really? I asked her when exactly I failed to mention something like this and she got up to shut the door because she said the conversation was getting out of hand. *But she never answered the question.* I asked her if she needed to know every time one of them is 10 minutes or 15 minutes late or if they're making time up at lunch or after work hours.

DISGRNTLD76: she says they're here after hours a lot and what are they doing here and am I aware of it? I answered that they were either finishing things or making time up and yes, I was aware of it.

2GR8T4wrk: ok

DISGRNTLD76: then she accused me of twisting her words and of seeing things only as "black or white" and that this was a "grey area"

DISGRNTLD76: So I asked her again, "Do you need to know every time they're late or making up time?"

DISGRNTLD76: she said "No - we just need better communication. If they're here after six o'clock, I'd like to know what they're working on."

2GR8T4wrk: so ask them

DISGRNTLD76: so then I asked her again, "Ok - so you want me to tell you when they're late and making up time?"

DISGRNTLD76: and she said, "you're twisting my words." and I said, "No - you're either asking the question or you aren't"

DISGRNTLD76: that's when she said that I was seeing things black or white only.

DISGRNTLD76: So I told her that this was a yes or no question - does she or doesn't she want me to tell her these details?

DISGRNTLD76: and she said to me, "well, you tell me when you're late and when you make up time." I said, "yeah - that's because you're a stickler for it."

2GR8T4wrk: that's a polite way of calling her a micromanager

DISGRNTLD76: I told her that *I* wasn't a stickler and that I was aware they tend to run in late but that they make their time up. I told her I spoke to them about their hours and the importance of them being here on time. Then I reminded her that the work was getting done and that's what mattered most to me -- I'm not the stickler.

DISGRNTLD76: she was pissed.

2GR8T4wrk: ha ha.

DISGRNTLD76: but we ended it w/me saying that I would talk to my team... again. was I wrong?

2GR8T4wrk: not only that, if you tell her about your time it's because she is your manager, that is who you should tell

2GR8T4wrk: they should tell you and that is enough. you're their manager.

DISGRNTLD76: that's what I said to her. she either wants to know or she doesn't

2GR8T4wrk: does she tell her boss so he can then tell his boss that you are making up time?

DISGRNTLD76: and she said No - we're a TEAM

DISGRNTLD76: I almost laughed in her face

2GR8T4wrk: no we in team

DISGRNTLD76: no s**t

DISGRNTLD76: so I asked her why she was getting questioned, and not me -- since they report to me. That's when she was all, "well we're a team"

2GR8T4wrk: you should have asked her for a trade

DISGRNTLD76: trade?

2GR8T4wrk: in sports players get traded from one team to another

DISGRNTLD76: yeah lol

2GR8T4wrk: many times at their request

DISGRNTLD76: I requested, remember? I got stuck

2GR8T4wrk: yeah

DISGRNTLD76: I mean, come ON -- this is nonsense.

2GR8T4wrk: yes it is.

DISGRNTLD76: I mean, she WAS asking to know their comings-and-goings, no?

2GR8T4wrk: She was - you can't do one without the other. you can't tell her what they're working on and when they are late without telling her that they are staying late because they came in late.

DISGRNTLD76: but she doesn't micromanage.

2GR8T4wrk: indeed.

"I'm Not a Micromanager!"

Oh really? How much do you want to bet that you're not? I cringed when I heard this story; it reminded me not only of similar stories I'd heard, but situations I'd been in. My friend Chris emailed this story to me:

"My lousy boss actually claimed that he was *not* a micromanager! He used that exact word too. He called me into his office for a meeting and closed the door behind me. I think that's a universal sign for I'm going to get an ass-kicking.

It turned out that this was a follow-up to a "discussion" that we had last Friday. The moron wanted to know why I missed the deadline for a quarterly report. It felt like déjà vu to me, but I went along for the ride anyhow.

Someone once told me that the only way to make your boss happy is to do your work the way that THEY would do it. Problems arise from individuals with differing work styles attempting to come together. Bottom line: at the end of the day it's not about you... it's about your boss. Make them happy and you'll be a superstar. Well, it only made sense to me.

So on that note, in last Friday's meeting, I had asked my manager for his suggestions on how I could approach my responsibilities better. I'm doing what I'm doing day-to-day and getting things done my way. But for some reason that's not making him happy. Forget about not being happy, the guy is outright pissed at me – and I don't know why! So as I said, I'm asking what it is that he's looking for, and asking for his recommendations on how best to go about getting it.

It would seem to me that if someone approaches you seeking your advice, you'd be flattered that they held you in high enough regard. I mean, they must want to hear what you have to say, no? Of course, since I want to make every day at work as minimally painful as possible, I want to know what he thinks.

Mind you, I don't *care* about what he thinks... I'm just trying to make my day-to-day work experience less painful than root canal.

Last Friday when I first asked him that question he stared blankly at me in response. Well, today when I asked the same question he actually gave me an answer. He said the things that worked for him were:

A-Working through lunchtime
B-Working late at night
C-Bringing work home
D-Working over the weekend

I should have asked him at what point he sacrifices his firstborn to the company.

Anyhow, when he told me this I just said that those were not good answers to "working better" or "working smarter". What he's suggesting is just "working longer". He had NO other suggestions on how to work better... no recommendations. What an idiot.

I'm at this company now a long time. For a solid chunk of that time I would come in early and stay late. On an average, I probably worked no less than ten hours a day. I used to bring work home and yes, I had come in over a weekend or two from time to time.

I will tell you what working overtime got me: Screwed.

At this point in our meeting today I told my manager that I had ZERO motivation for working beyond my scheduled hours of 9 to 6. It's almost three years since I've had a raise, five-and-a-half years since I had a promotion, my yearly bonuses are practically non-existent; when at my level, they should be "cushy" and on top of all that, the annual reviews are vague at best. When I approached HR about my situation, they said nothing, although they made it clear that they completely back the manager.

Isn't this the kind of company you'd want to work for every day?

So I more or less told him that overtime was over. However, I also told him that in an emergency I would stay. Just last night I stayed until 7:30 p.m. (and considering that I don't work overtime anymore, this was late).

When I told him that I wouldn't stay after hours anymore, he told me that it made me a bad manager. Of course, coming from him it means nothing.

Getting back to what I said before about making your boss happy – if you can do this, great. You should always try to go the path of working with someone... or at least be willing to do so. If you're working for human beings, this method ought to work.

It's my rotten luck that I don't work for human beings.

If you find yourself in a situation like mine, bang your head against a brick wall. Then repeat the motion. If at all possible, bang your idiot boss' head against a brick wall and repeat. That might make you feel better."

When I later repeated this story to another friend of mine, she had this to say:

"To quote the soon to be ex-president of my division at work, "You're a good manager when your job becomes obsolete". Hence, when you hire intelligent, motivated people, there is absolutely no $#@%'ing need to be up their ass. Keep in mind that this particular gentleman is climbing his way up the corporate ladder of the Walt Disney Company and will be probably be running the entire corporation in a few years.

All I see your boss running is a sweatshop in Indonesia. Who put this person in charge of actual people? He really belongs in a corner, (make that the basement) of a building, and should only be allowed up for crackers & water once a day!"

31 Emails

One time when I returned from an extended holiday weekend, I found thirty-one emails in my Inbox from my bat-$#@%-crazy manager. This was over the course of two-and-a-half days.

Almost every one of these emails required a response.

This boss was also a Supreme Micromanager. I've read several books on successful management skills and this guy did not possess one of these skills. In one of the books I read, one way to throw "The Micromanager" off-course is to send as many emails as possible their way. They'll have so much email to go through it'll rattle their cage and they won't know how to respond.

I have the answer: STEP AWAY FROM THE EMAIL!!! EMAIL IS <u>NOT</u> THE ANSWER.

Warning:

If your boss is a Supreme Micromanager, they will not only respond to every one of your emails, they will send TWO for every ONE that you sen

This is not a joke and should not be tried unless your schedule is cleared for the remainder of the year. If you have a job that leaves you nothing to do, then by all means go ahead and entertain yourself. However, if this is what you consider to be entertainment, then you need to find a life.

Take it from me: these people take email seriously. It has become a dangerous addiction for them. What makes it worse is that there's nothing you can do to win in this situation.

Possible courses of action:

1: If feasible, condense your responses into ONE email... although I didn't have much success with that one personally.

2: If you can, ignore the emails as long as humanly possible and continue with your work as planned. Chances are, these individuals have clogged your Inboxes with inane questions, worthless tidbits of data, and usually repeat themselves ad nauseam. Besides, if you ignore them it will probably drive them mad – which if nothing else, may make you feel better.

3: If they call you and ask if you've seen their emails – and why you haven't answered them, you should respond, "Yes I have seen the messages, and it looks like you have more to add to a growing list of topics that I already don't care about." Then print them all out and suggest a meeting to address them in person. If this is someone who is email-crazy, a face-to-face meeting might throw them off.

Give it a try. If you're like me, you have nothing to lose. Then again, I hope you're not like me with an idiot boss! I wouldn't wish that on my worst enemy.

INSUBORDINATION (a.k.a. Being Cheeky)

I've almost completely overlooked this topic! Let's take a look at insubordination. What is it?

"Insubordination *may be described as resistance to or defiance of authority, disobedience, refusal or failure to obey reasonable and lawful instructions, insolence, cheekiness, rudeness, brining the employer's name into disrepute, and rebellious or mutinous behavior resulting in an actual work stoppage.*"

So what is it really? Every instance I've read about maintains that it is an employee's willful disregard of an employer's directive. It is also suggested that "inappropriate" language may sometimes (ahem) accompany the insubordinate behavior.

It is cautioned: In cases of abusive language, consider the context in which the incident occurred. An employee is more likely to be found to have engaged in insubordination if the abusive language:

- was not provoked by the supervisor
- was spoken in the presence of other employees or customers
- was not an example of shop talk in the workplace

So how is it OK for a supervisor to *provoke* an outburst in an employee but then write that employee up for insubordination? What I'm getting at here, bottom-line, is that something needs to be done about this. If employees need to watch their P's and Q's with management, why is it okay for management to walk all over their employees? *How very cheeky of them.*

Then when the employees approach HR for support, HR hangs them out to dry and frankly, the employee has no other good option but to find a job elsewhere. This needs to change. I understand that life isn't fair, but I just hear way too many instances of these things happening.

What's the point?

Communication... managers need to learn how it works. Long gone are the days where we simply do what we are told. Now, at best, we need to repeat what our bosses say, write it down, and follow it up with an email. And that STILL gives us no guarantee that our bat-$#@%-crazy manager isn't going to turn around and clobber us with, "That's not what I told you to do!"

Also, it would help if they knew *how* to explain what needs to be done. It's great that they know what they're doing, but if I have to ask you four times to restate it differently, that means you need to find a better way to go about it. This is just reality.

In order to avoid this, what I've done is write up extensive "How-to" manuals that literally take a person by the hand on what needs to get done for every task. If anyone finds a better way to perform step number three than as I've laid it out, by all means go for it. Or, if something needs further clarification, I go back and re-write it. I have never done a manual from start to finish on my own. If there are others that need it, then it needs to pass their inspection.

Let's face it; sometimes someone else has a better way to phrase things. But it helps to learn some of these ways and use them. It makes better managers and helps shape future leaders. I'm just saying.

Lesson learned:

Don't sweat the small stuff – for both parties. Something is always going to happen. We need to deal with that. Chances are, there's going to be things that drive us mad about our bosses. It's just the way it is. Pick and choose your battles smartly. Let the small stuff go. You'll have to or you'll go mad.

On the other hand, they need to chill as well. Mistakes are not the end of the world. Sometimes, mistakes are needed in order to move forward or do things more efficiently in the future. If there's a mistake, like you left off a comma in a ten page memo to a group, this is not a tragedy. There's a big difference between mistakes like that and several grammatical issues that alter the meaning of a message, or the same mistakes over and over.

My big thing was always: is the work correct? If yes, then get over the fact that I failed to bold a word on page 399, or left out a set of parentheses where there should be a set. It was a mistake. Let me know about it, I'll fix it and won't do it again next time.

If I make repeated mistakes however, that may be a little different. But still, it's not as though I'm failing to report millions of dollars in company liability due to a glitch in the system that I should have caught. I mean, that's something that could (and should) lead to termination. But commas, font style and color? Boss please... let me get back to work.

CHAPTER SIX

If You Can't Say Anything Nice, At Least Say It With Flourish

"I find it rather easy to portray a businessman. Being bland, rather cruel and incompetent comes naturally to me." - *John Cleese*

During one of my annual reviews a while back, I had a bat-$#@%-crazy manager who said many things to me. One of them was that I lacked the expertise required to fulfill my role. She was referring to a previous role in which I had worked until the year prior. Same title, different (better) area of the department.

When I asked her for an example she came up empty. "Well," she said, "you don't show strength in your responsibilities. *You're not the expert at what you do.*"

Hel-lo??? I helped to create the job I was in and built it from the ground level up. I conducted research, informational interviews, wrote policy, gave presentations and trained company employees across the country. It was all done to develop a new area of the department. I did that job for five years. I was a pioneer.

Yet, I lacked the expertise. How was that possible?

I continued to ask for an example and she continued to come up empty.

After that initial meeting, I collected my documentation. In it, I included my presentations, the list of reports I created, the processes I put in place and last – but not least – dozens of thank-you notes and various commendations from the many individuals I brushed shoulders with on a daily basis. There were a total of about thirty commendations taken over a six-month period of time.

When I brought the documentation into my next meeting with the idiot boss, she called me "inappropriate" for including the commendations. Then I told her that she was "inappropriate" for saying that I was "inept" in my job and not providing so much as one example where I fell short.

Then my behavior was considered insubordinate and I got into a lot of trouble. Let me tell you, you can be 100% right and still be 100% fired.

Well, I didn't get fired. But I never got an answer either. What a fun job that was.

The Ultimate Insult: a.k.a. - The Yearly Review

I came across an article that piqued my interest entitled, "Can You Redeem Yourself After a Bad Review at Work?" I read stuff like this that seems to make all the sense in the world. And then I wonder - why can't I have it like that? Why can't we *all* have it like that?

Let's take a look at some of the tips offered in regards to your annual review:

Ask for specifics. The best way to improve your performance is if you know what you are doing wrong. Ask your manager to spell out exactly where you are lacking so you can make improvements. If he or she simply says that you "don't seem to be motivated" in the office, respectfully ask for examples of where and when you have fallen short. This will help you see things from your manager's perspective.

Reality:
Performance reviews can be scary for most people. They're scary because they either never know what their supervisor will say or they're simply afraid of what they'll say. I doubt that Lynn's story is unique:

"I guess your manager isn't necessarily required to supply any specifics. One time I had a particularly lousy review. I waited and waited for answers and never got them. My manager was unable to produce even one example of anything that I did "wrong".

One of the things that she said to me was, "Your subordinate, Worker Smith, came to me on several occasions to complain about you."

Oh really?

So I asked my boss what it was that Worker Smith said about me. After all, if they went to my manager "on several occasions" to complain, surely she could remember one thing that they said? Why were they complaining and what could I have done to remedy that situation?

My bat-$@%#-crazy manager turned white and tried to think of something to say.

Hmmm, what an odd reaction.

So I asked, "Would you tell me at least one thing that they said? You just told me that Worker Smith came to you on several occasions. What was the complaint?" How can I improve if I don't know what needs improving?

She struggled for an answer, "I don't seem to remember anything offhand at this time."

"Okay, then why don't we call Worker Smith in here? Since you don't seem to be able to recall what was said, maybe we can hear it from the horse's mouth, no? If this is a negative mark against me, I think I have the right to know what they said."

Apparently the idiot saw that as unnecessary. Really? Then maybe that shouldn't be in my review. As I said, she did not come up with even one item of complaint that Worker Smith went to her with. (When I later approached Worker Smith and asked what the complaints were, the individual denied ever having such a conversation with my manager. W.S. went on to say how I mentored and supported their goals all along. This, of course, was documented, though played no role in the defense of my reputation. Hmmm.)"

Understand expectations. Sometimes, being a star at work is all about expectations. You need to understand your manager's idea of "outstanding" or "meets expectations" in order to meet them. Ask your manager to give you examples of accomplishments or behaviors that are required to earn a better evaluation.

Reality:
In Chris' case earlier, he asked his manager what he needed to do. He got a terrible answer. His boss told him to work lots of overtime. The exact words were: "work through lunchtime, work late at night, bring work home and work weekends." Now how can anyone realistically meet those expectations?

Set clear and attainable goals. The best way to show that you are improving is to set goals and meet those goals. With your supervisor's help develop a list of short- and long-term goals that go along with the areas in your review. This will demonstrate that you are committed to improvement and will give you a road map to follow.

Reality:
Having goals is crucial to meeting expectations. If those goals are not given out, or given out too late in the year, it does not

allow employees a shot at getting it right. Beyond that, the goals need to be clear, and attainable.

Don't go it alone. If you find that you need assistance, ask for it. Maybe you just haven't gotten the hang of the new accounting system or are having troubles managing a certain client. If you don't step up and ask for help, your work - and your career - will continue to suffer.

Reality:
I was once "restructured" (a.k.a. put in a job that I didn't want). Nobody thoroughly trained me, although I repeatedly asked for training. My subordinates at that time trained me instead. Their mistakes then became my mistakes which I got in trouble for. Finally, when the mistakes mounted, I was placed on written warning. Only then did management deem it time to thoroughly train me in my new role. Nice, right?

Meet regularly. If the only time you sit down with your boss is at your annual review, it may be difficult for you to improve much in the workplace. You need to build a relationship with your manager that provides you with ongoing support and feedback. If necessary, set up meetings every few weeks to talk about your goals and discuss your progress.

Reality:
There are some bat-$@%#-crazy managers that require daily meetings. This does not mean that they should use the opportunity to make their subordinates feel worse about things they didn't even think were possible to feel bad about. Yet it happens.

Keep a record. The workplace has a short memory and a performance review is normally conducted just once a year. That's why it is important for you to keep a file of your accomplishments throughout the year. Share these with your supervisor as he prepares your performance appraisal to remind him of your achievements.

Reality:

Documentation does nothing. After Lynn's miserable review, she went to Inhuman Resources to see what they could possibly do. She had plenty of good reviews in the past and did not want this to mar her otherwise fine reputation. She pulled all of her documentation together and made a case for herself. It included everything that said not only that she did her job – but that she did it well. Her documentation included memos and emails from several individuals in the company (some of them upper management) who commended her on a "job well done". Long story short – Inhuman Resources told her nothing. The review would stand. According to Lynn, they never even looked at the documentation. Screw documentation.

It is as a result of all this sort of nonsense that I decided to quit my job, quit my industry and start my own company. Lynn is not alone in the corporate world. I can relate well to what she says. Believe me, I would never have struck out on my own if I saw companies operate the way they were supposed to (or at least as they claim they do). I know I'm not alone in this. Maybe in a way this is a sign that we should be doing bigger and better things. We'll have to see.

<u>Performance Mismanagement</u>

Since I've had performance management on the brain, I decided to address it. The following is the "Performance Management Process Checklist" that I found in an article written by Susan M. Heathfield for About.com. In it, Susan clearly defines how performance reviews *should* proceed. Unfortunately, life seldom works out that way. At least at my job it didn't.

I address each checklist point with translations on what really goes on:

1) Define the purpose of the job, job duties, and responsibilities.
What They Mean:
We're going to make your life miserable.

2) Define performance goals with measurable outcomes.
What They Mean:
This is not a hard job to do. To make it more challenging, we will throw up roadblocks at every opportunity so that you do not achieve any of your goals. We have made fulfilling your responsibilities an Olympic event; very few (if any) have ever survived and those that have now live in padded cells.

3) Define the priority of each job responsibility and goal.
What They Mean:
Every last function of the job that you perform is a priority. How you choose to define your priorities is up to you; however, regardless of what you do, it will be wrong. If you submit Report A, we will have wanted Report B, even though we didn't ask for it. Thanks for playing, please try your luck again next time.

4) Define performance standards for key components of the job.
What They Mean:
Although the tasks as we state them sound easy enough to accomplish, we will set you up for failure. We tell you to come to us with any questions and when you do, we reserve the right to 1) Not answer you at all or, 2) Give you a wrong answer. It is up to our discretion, as our mood sees fit. You are only here for our amusement.

5) Hold interim discussions and provide feedback about employee performance, preferably daily, summarized and discussed, at least, quarterly. (Provide positive and constructive feedback.)
What They Mean:

We will hold daily floggings. It's positive and constructive for us. You do not matter.

6) Maintain a record of performance through critical incident reports. (Jot notes about contributions or problems throughout the quarter, in an employee file.)
What They Mean:
This is where we get to make up stuff about you and be as general as possible. It doesn't matter that you have documentation to prove otherwise. If you try to go against us, we will get our Inhuman Resources department to back us up, since we keep them in our back pockets anyway.

7) Provide the opportunity for broader feedback. Use a 360 degree performance feedback system that incorporates feedback from the employee's peers, customers, and people who may report to him.
What They Mean:
We don't care what anyone else thinks or says that's positive about you. What we say goes. It could be inaccurate or an outright lie. That's how we roll.

8) Develop and administer a coaching and improvement plan if the employee is not meeting expectations.
What They Mean:
We will place you on written warning if you attempt to have independent thoughts. If you do not cease and desist, we will place you on probation. If, at that time we just don't want you around anymore, we will terminate your employment. We don't need anyone around with better ideas who will - or already has - made us look bad.

Performance Review Etiquette

The whole point of the review is to sum up your job performance from the previous year. Sounds like a simple idea, but for some reason it gets turned inside-out so easily.

This is a good opportunity for our supervisors to make or break us. Unfortunately, there are just so many of those individuals out there that are out to cut others down. I never understood why treating others this way makes these people feel better. If that was me, I'd have night terrors over it until I reconciled the wrongs.

I certainly don't think I'm naïve and I certainly don't think I'm "righteous". In this situation I'm just "right".

One of my blog readers emailed me this story:

"So I had my yearly review. While it was an improvement over last year's, it still contained unwarranted and incorrect comments about my performance. Many of the remarks were just not based in reality. Sadly, though I can prove I'm right, Inhuman Resources will do nothing to help me. So I have to live with more marks against my good name.

In a way it's amazing. I was discussing my review with a friend and commenting that while my bat-$#@%-crazy manager's remarks started off "positive", they all ended up as an under-handed insult. Each one of them. It's almost an art; a lot of thought had to go into that."

What's the point?

Performance management should be used by your manager as a guide for their staff to accomplish set goals. It allows for your manager to let you know where you stand on meeting your goals and where there is room for improvement. It should also only be one part of a series of such meetings held throughout the year for this purpose.

Managers should be well prepped before signing anyone's death warrant, I mean, yearly review. They need to know – in advance – what they're going to say, how to say it *properly*, and how best to answer questions they will be asked by their subordinates.

Lesson learned:

This is not a forum for a manager to air personal grievances. If you're going to go on the record about someone's performance, you'd better be damn sure you can back that up with examples and specifics. This is only fair. If you fail to do so it will only serve to add insult to injury as well as set the employee up for future failures since they (in your feeble opinion) don't know what you expect of them. They can only improve if you tell them exactly where they need work and what they need to do. Draw them a map if you have to.

Nobody goes into their review hoping that they've screwed you over by not performing their responsibilities (unless they're deranged). If you're going to go to the point where you actually insult their intelligence, you'd be better be prepared for the consequences.

CHAPTER SEVEN

Influence With a Large Hammer

"In the business world, the rearview mirror is always clearer than the windshield." - *Warren Buffett*

Management is a people-based liberal art. Peter Drucker, who is known as the "father of modern management", commented on his long life before he passed away at the age of 95. Summing it up, he said that he "looked at people, not buildings or machines." The man was an innovator and widely respected as THE authority on management.

So how is it that corporate practices have strayed so far from his idea? In theory, more rules and laws and company handbooks scrutinize every angle by which people are accountable to the company they work for and in turn, the things the company may and may not do to the employee.

Yet there are many aspects to this business that remind me of days years back, that I contemplated pursuing a career in the music industry. I was a hardcore music fanatic and worked at my college radio station as a music director for almost four years. At the very end when I needed to make up my mind, I decided against taking an offer to work at a record label because the business struck me as unseemly. If I only knew what I was getting into on the "proper" end. No one warns college seniors that there are many businesses that are unseemly. Don't get me wrong; I'm sure that most businesses in and of themselves are honorable and legitimate. It's just that jobs in those businesses should come with warning labels about politics and "dirty pool". Ya dig?

Well let me tell you something: "proper" boils down to what each individual's threshold for pain is. One man's poison is another man's fodder. At this point I'll never know what would have been working at a label. I do know that what may seem the "proper" path to take, may not be proper at all.

Lead By Example

Just what exactly would happen if employees performed their job responsibilities based on their managers' examples?

Let's see…

If you lack self-confidence:

- Chances are you'd gang up on subordinates and coworkers then beat them to a pulp so that you could make yourself feel better.

- You'd find something wrong with anything and everything that anyone else did.

If you don't care:

- No amount of pleas from others will make you stop. As a matter of fact, you will probably have the support of *your* idiot manager and they will want you to continue this way.

If you don't experience negative consequences:

- As long as you have the backing of *your* moron boss, chances are that Inhuman Resources will back you too. After all, wolves travel in packs, right?

If you have psychological problems:

- Well, I suppose some of these can be learned from enough exposure in the "right" surroundings.

If you're a micromanager:

- Then you too will scrutinize every email for correct comma placement, use of bullet points, and font size.

- Status reports will become the norm so that you can know every move your subordinates make, even in and out of the restroom.

Come on, doesn't this sound like the kind of manager you'd want to be? The good news is, there are plenty of mentors like this out in the corporate world. One only has to open their eyes to witness it firsthand at every turn. So sleep tight, following their examples could very easily get you promoted... just you wait and see!

Don't Kill Creativity!!!

I once left a job and some very bright subordinates behind. They were hired because of their backgrounds, experience, and because they struck me as smart tacks that could get the job done. Granted, the job wasn't rocket science, but - as with most jobs, there needs to be a certain amount of ambition and drive to go beyond what is expected. This is how people succeed and move forward in their careers. At least it's one way to do that.

From the time they started, they demonstrated a strong ability to pick things up quickly and execute them. I trained them and gave them highly detailed "How-To" sheets and let them run with them. They got the basics down and started looking to "step up to the plate" and pick up some more responsibilities. I was so proud of them. I showed them how to do things one time and they wanted a little bit of space to try it for themselves. People learn differently and this is what they asked for, so I let them do what they were comfortable with.

I was nervous about how they would do when I departed. Not because I thought they'd falter, but because I was afraid they wouldn't be *allowed* to do their jobs.

This brings me to the subject of **letting go**.

It's important for managers to trust and let their employees do their jobs. Good managers allow their staff a certain amount of freedom to go about fulfilling their responsibilities. For starters, it's empowering and builds self-esteem. When people feel good about their jobs they become motivated. Just a note: **YOU WANT MOTIVATED EMPLOYEES!!!**

Aside from that, if you allow your staff that freedom it gives them the chance to be creative. Suppose they come up with a better, more efficient way of doing something? In my book, if your staff can accomplish tasks like this, it's going to make you, the manager, look like a hero.

Another note: Mistakes are not the enemy! Sometimes mistakes can be good - smart people learn from them. Doing things differently also keeps the creativity alive and can keep business thriving. You have to allow some room for it.

An insecure and untrusting bat-$#%@-crazy manager is capable of doing the following:

-Stifling any and all motivation and creativity that employees currently bring to the table.

-Correcting their emails for punctuation (i.e.: harassment over comma placement).

-Nit-picking about formatting issues on reports ("No, I want it in BOLD and 10point Times New Roman!!!").

-Belittling them for any/every little mistake.

-Watching their comings-and-goings while keeping a keen eye on the clock ("You were five minutes late today, I want to know how you're going to make that up.").

-Setting them up for failure.

-Falsely accusing of them of poor performance.

-Making their lives a living hell.

This is not "good manager" behavior. This is (very) "bad manager" behavior. This is Miss Manager behavior.

Don't be a mismanager.

Return of the Workplace Bully: Thank you, Mr. Expert

It's interesting how the "experts" say that bullies at work *project* their shortcomings and inadequacies upon their victim. Each time a bully does this, they in short, reveal tidbits about themselves.

You know, this is all fine and good. However, if I'm getting ripped a "new one" by my boss, I'm not allowing for a moment to celebrate the fact that I now know something about them that I probably already knew: **THEY'RE BAT-$#@%-CRAZY!!!** I don't need some expert telling me that this person is incompetent, stupid, self-obsessed, a moron... whatever, you get the point.

Thank you, Mr. Expert. Tell me something I DON'T already know.

Are You Asking For It?

I read an article titled, "The Dangers of Being a Micromanager". In it, the author says that some employees tend to want to be micromanaged.

Oh, really? – you might be saying. Let's take a look at this. What are some reasons why some supervisors micromanage?

1. *The manager has an obsessive/compulsive need to be in control.* Trust me on this one, there is no way that an employee wants to be caught in this mess. It is an outright ugly and demeaning situation to find oneself in. The manager will not change but rather make your life miserable. Get into another department or look for another job.

2. ***There is a lack of trust in the relationship***. There could be a few reasons this occurs. Maybe the employee did something that questions their ability to get the job done and the supervisor is required to step in. The other reason could be one that stems from #1: if the manager needs to be in control, they will never trust anyone to step in to do the job as well as they can. While this may or may not be the case, it does nothing to foster the subordinate's self-confidence to be able to do the job. It causes doubt and then people are miserable on all sides. Not a good place to be in.

3. ***The subordinate is not capable of making any decisions on their own***. This is the only scenario that has a shot at being valid for micromanaging. Believe me, I'm not saying that this is right… I'm only giving a nod that this happens and may not be the manager's fault.

So you need to ask yourself: Who is this person that I hired that cannot convey a complete thought without my help? Chances are, if you hired them, they have at least half a brain to do the job.

Have they been thoroughly trained? Perhaps the questions stem from confusion over how to complete certain tasks. Revisit these things as appropriate.

Are they making the same mistakes over and over? Perhaps they don't understand the job properly or maybe they're just not cut out for the work. If after some coaching, the individual still shows zero aptitude for their job responsibilities, it may be time to cut the ties and set them free. Hopefully, they'll see that the relationship isn't working out and agree to an amicable split.

However, through all of that, not once do I get an image in my head that anyone is going to want to be micromanaged. There's a big difference between asking a question for help and not knowing how to do the job.

If the employee seeks constant reinforcement on the same issues, then it is the manager's job to properly mentor the employee and foster and a strong working relationship. Sometimes people need to be encouraged to make changes and accept accountability. If the person is that insecure about doing the job, then it really needs to be asked if their career goals are realistic. It may be time to shift gears and try something else.

Don't baby sit your staff. Trust me – they don't want it.

Got Motivation?

Be what you want to see. In other words, lead by example. Don't ask your subordinates or colleagues that which you are not willing to do yourself.

Don't criticize management. This is certainly not a way to motivate others. People need to believe they're doing something for a bigger cause. If they see that cause as pointless, they will do less and morale will plummet.

Be present (a.k.a. do the one thing). This will at least give the illusion that you have things in order. Also, if subordinates see you spinning out of control, they will feel that you **A:** don't have time for them and/or **B:** cannot fully back them.

Know your people's strengths. Knowing what they're good at and capitalizing on it will not only make you look good, it will boost the team's morale.

10 Tips for Performing Under Pressure

As you can probably tell by now, I like to do a lot of reading. This is due to the fact that I'm searching for The Answer. So far, I've come across interesting bits of advice, though I have yet to come across the definitive Answer on how to deal with crazy managers and coworkers.

Today's corporate world is fast-paced and deadline-driven. Many companies have not yet fully recovered from the economic downturn and are still operating on tight budgets and lean staff levels. Employees across the board are managing large workloads and long hours. *On top of that, many employees have rotten managers.*

As a result, now more than ever, on-the-job success depends on your ability to show grace under fire. Anyhow, I found this article that offers ten tips to help you become a peak performer when the pressure's on and you have a moron manager. As usual, this did not pass without my own remarks which follow each tip, in *italics*:

1. Go with the flow.

Adaptability is an invaluable skill. If priorities change and your boss asks you to move from one project to another, embrace the new challenge and demonstrate your ability to learn on the fly. Remember: If you're always flexible, you'll never get bent out of shape.

However, what that can also mean is: If you have a boss who is disorganized and doesn't even know how to manage so much as an ant farm, they will give a list of tasks as long as your arm and then tear you away to do other meaningless projects. Once you've gone along with them and allowed them to derail you, they will then wonder why you didn't get the first list done and berate you for it. Sometimes you need to put your foot down – if you're asked to do something that doesn't make sense... speak up!

2. Seek clarity.

Don't be afraid of asking too many questions. If a hot assignment is dropped in your lap with little warning, it's to your advantage to clarify timelines, personal expectations and overall goals with your manager before starting work.

What will happen: Even if you have half a brain, a micromanaging moron will send you eighty-eight emails explaining how to arrange the proper subject header of an email. Sometimes there is such a thing as too much "clarity". Tell your bat-$#@%-crazy manager to "lead, follow, or get out of the way".

3. Prioritize, then strategize.

Take a few moments to develop a game plan before diving headfirst into any project. By thinking tactically and constructing a road map on the front end, you can spot potential hurdles before they slow you down. A plan will also help you stay clear-headed throughout the process.

Regardless of how well you plan, an idiot boss will do their best (often without trying) to block your best efforts to get your job done. Then they will lecture you about how to manage your time better (i.e. working through lunch, staying late, bringing work home and working weekends... and let's not forget the sacrificial first-born).

4. Don't procrastinate.

Worrying about a project doesn't count as working on it. Rather than putting off your most pressing deadlines, hop to it. Getting these assignments out of the way first will lower your stress level and make your overall goals seem more manageable.

(See point #3)

5. Break it up.

Take short breaks to relieve crunch-time tension. Collect your thoughts by going for a walk, stretching or briefly engaging in water cooler chitchat. If you can't leave your workstation, close your eyes, take some deep breaths and try to clear your head for a few moments.

If you worked in my office there was almost no socializing allowed. You had to be chained to your desk. It sounds like good advice just to take deep breaths, but sometimes the only thing that helps is getting fresh air. What's even better is hanging your boss out of a seventh story window by their feet so that they too can join you in the fresh air. Now that's teamwork!

6. Stay cool.

Even the most affable and well-mannered people can become flustered and temperamental when under stress. Don't contribute to the tense atmosphere. Although it's not always easy, take criticism with a grain of salt on hectic days. Think before speaking and don't let anyone else's poor attitude affect your own.

I have learned this one the hard way. Relax! If you know you've done the best job possible, then that is enough. If someone else doesn't appreciate that (and if they never will), then it's certainly best for you to move past it and let it go. Trust me on this one.

7. Ask for help.

Even with talent and a Herculean effort, some jobs simply can't be completed by one person. If you're doing everything possible to accomplish a task and still foresee a problem, ask for assistance. Identify duties that can be delegated and request backup from your supervisor. He or she would much rather divert resources to help you now than hear of a missed deadline later.

Not if you had my managers!!! I actually received resentment over getting help on projects in the past – especially one time in particular when I was down two employees on my team (and therefore handling the workload of three people). I had to "step up to the plate", but no one else did. Hmmm.

8. Fix your gaze.

When operating on overdrive, it's easy to lose sight of big-picture goals and the fact that working hard now will help you achieve them. Keep your eye on the light at the end of the tunnel.

Sometimes the light at the end of the tunnel is the vision of your gasoline-drenched bat-$#@%-crazy manager meeting a lit match.

9. Turn downtime into prep time.
After a high-intensity period passes, decompress by making note of the lessons you just learned. What factors, if any, caused you to fall off schedule? If leading a project team, how could you have communicated goals more effectively? Reflective thinking will help you streamline your pressure-handling processes and prepare you for the next big brush fire.

"Reflective" time may be when you realize that you're going nowhere fast working for an idiot that's making you sick and you need to get the hell outta Dodge!!! Downtime could be a great time to work on your resume – at home, of course.

10. Foster good office karma.
It's always a smart move to build rapport with co-workers. If a colleague is on deadline and has an inbox piled to the ceiling, offer to help if you can. By lending a hand, you'll likely make an ally who'll return the favor the next time you're in a pinch.

That is, unless you work in an office that does not foster a friendly environment... then you're pretty much on your own.

To perform well when the heat is on and the stakes are high, you need focus, organization, and steely resolve (*as well as the absence of a bat-$#@%-crazy manager*). Being optimistic and viewing challenges as opportunities for growth won't hurt either (*but of course that can be beaten out of you*). Use the tips highlighted above to not just survive but thrive the next time you find yourself under the gun.

What's the point?

As a manager, think of all the things you do every day. Now, think of all the things that you ask of your staff and expect them to do for you and the company every day. Did you do that? Good... now throw all of that stuff out the window.

In many ways, a manager serves as representation of the company's values. You need to remember that as you berate a subordinate for being two minutes late and just why exactly are they balancing their checkbook at their desk two minutes after the end of the day? This sets up an environment of mistrust. Once the trust in a work relationship – or any relationship – is gone, it will take a lot of work to get it back. Besides, your staff will begin to think you're nuts. If you go on this way, or micromanage without reason, they'll actually be right. If your staff knows their job, there should be no reason to micromanage. Ever.

Lesson learned:

It *is* possible to do the right thing. Get over yourself and trust your employees. Believe me, they want to trust you. But if you keep doing stupid things, this will never happen. Holding their hand over everyday tasks is demeaning. They will resent you for it. After that, the creativity will cease. Then, in order to get anything done, you will need to intimidate them and make outrageous demands. Eventually, they'll be exhausted and shell shocked and just look for employment elsewhere. If you really don't care, then continue to do this. Otherwise, suffer the fate of countless voodoo dolls with pins through the eyes and spleen.

CHAPTER EIGHT

Those Who Throw Dirt Are Sure to Lose Ground.

"An office with many people and few electrical outlets could be in for a power struggle." - *Unknown*

Office Politics

It's tough to hang in there with a job where office politics run rampant. While it's something that cannot often be avoided, there are ways to survive.

For starters, remember Mom's advice: *Keep your nose clean.* Don't get caught up in office gossip. If you're smart you certainly won't be the one starting it. But if it's your manager(s) that is instigating it, tread carefully. I was once caught in a situation where one of my managers made disparaging comments about a coworker. While this person was of no consequence to me, I was careful not to agree or disagree with the remarks. It's a good idea to tactfully change the topic of conversation to something more neutral.

One thing to think about, though, if you find yourself in this situation; be cognizant of your own words and deeds. If your manager can rip your coworker apart behind their back, they can do it to you as well.

Again, that's a situation I found myself in. Whether it's true or not is irrelevant; what they think *is*. Your boss can be completely wrong about you and yet they can still wreck your reputation.

Someone once told me about a conversation between my managers where they had discussed my personal affairs.

Unfortunately, it was a case where I heard it second-hand and was unable to address it directly with them (particularly because it would have incriminated the individual who told me). If I'd heard it myself I could have taken the bull by the horns. However, I couldn't.

The only thing to really do in that situation is to be beyond reproach. Don't give anyone any reason to give credence to the gossip they're spreading. Do the job you were hired to do. Show up on time and work as hard as you know you can. Continue to produce the results as you were before and conduct yourself as professionally as possible. It may be killing you to not say anything, but the more you act contrary to their beliefs, they *may* one day give it up.

Of course, that's not what happened with me. But I was sure to watch my "P's" and "Q's". I gave my managers nothing to go on, but they still came up with things that were pulled out of thin air. I only wish I knew what they were thinking.

I give this advice because I know there is the possibility of succeeding in other work environments. It *is* possible to play their game. Unfortunately, I can make no guarantees.
Let me follow up with some rules.

Rules of Engagement

As promised, the following are some rules you'll need to arm yourselves with in order to play the office politics game. It can be looked at two ways. One, play by the rules and get "in" or two, screw the rules and do what's best for you, or you can just have some plain old fun.

Help the people you work with! I've said this before; make your boss look good, you'll be a superstar. Or, help your subordinates and your bat-$@#%-crazy manager will promote them over you. Either way, it's a winner.

Try to do projects that put you on people's radars. Of course, if you have to look for the "high profile" work, chances are it's gone. I mean, do you really think that anything THAT important isn't already being reported to the decision makers? There's always a load of the bulls*** work left over. Always enough of that to go around. Get buried sufficiently in that and your moron manager will start asking for your red Swingline stapler.

"Love thy neighbor, but pick thy neighborhood." I love this quote. Choose your friends wisely. It is as valuable now as it was in grade school. Unfortunately, many people at this "professional" level still act like they were in grade school. So okay, maybe it's not the wisest move to befriend an obvious slacker, but sometimes people aren't liked just "because". So you have to not like them too? That's right! Screw 'em – sell yourself out to the highest bidder.

Avoid negativity. I love this one! It's easy enough to do when the negativity isn't happening to you. If it is, well... roll with it. That is until the acid reflux, depression, and anxiety get so bad that you just need to do what I did and that is look for another job!

Cultivate good relationships with others in your company. This is always advisable. Do what you can to make others' lives easier. Know everything you can know about your job that will help others. That way when you need those people, they can in turn give you great references to get out from under the Evil Empire, uh, I mean your own bosses. On a serious note, cultivating the right relationships with the peons today will mean you have vice presidents and leaders as your friends tomorrow.

Develop social savvy – but be careful of what you do in front of coworkers, even when socializing. This is another great one, but can backfire just as easily. I've been friends with those held "in high regard" who have been caught doing the dumbest things and they emerge unscathed, meanwhile I'll be the one coming out smelling like well, you know. Then of course, I was friends with someone who got so totally piss drunk at a company function and then turned around and got promoted. There's no real rhyme or reason to this one.

Confidences are almost always broken. This is an important one. Guard your secrets like Fort Knox. It doesn't matter who you trust or how much they swear they will never tell another soul… this one will almost always come back to haunt you. Don't tell people anything you don't want known.

These are just some of the guidelines I can think of. As I come across more, I'll be sure to share them. Office politics is a funny thing. Sometimes it just boils down to being in the right place at the right time. You can play your cards right and still wind up the loser.

Icksnay on the egativityNay

One of the greatest things I ever heard while working in an office was, *"Don't be drawn into the negativity"*.

This is what this says to me:

"We know we've done some reprehensible things to people here. Even though these people didn't deserve to be treated so unfairly (and really, who does?), you should not feel sorry for them. As a matter of fact, you shouldn't feel anything at all. Come see us for pointers, we're experts at it."

It's one thing to say "don't gossip", but it's another when something shameful happens, rather publicly I might add, to an individual and you're told to look the other way. This isn't just about "keeping your nose clean". This is like the German civilians looking the other way while the Nazis slaughtered millions of innocent people. Okay, so it's not as dramatic – but you get my point, right? What would you think of your boss if you knew they screwed over an innocent co-worker or subordinate? Even if you kept quiet about it, I'm thinking you'd probably not have any nice thoughts about them in your mind.

So in this type of scenario: **How would you stay away from the negativity?** I mean, you could be next!

Pie In The Sky?

Telecommuting is a nice idea for a lot of people. Companies institute this practice as a benefit for employees to help cut down their commutes, and to show flexibility for a positive work-life balance. Some of the best companies employ such programs.

However, not all companies allow for telecommuting. Granted, not every job can be done from the comfort of one's home. So right there we can't question why everyone isn't "doing it". For those companies that have it and allow employees the benefit to work from home, there are still individuals who are *not allowed* this privilege. Let's look at some reasons why some managers shoot those people down:

1: The subordinate's job truly isn't flexible enough to allow it. While the benefit and capability may be there, the job may be too volatile to rely on a fixed schedule of being away from the office. If the job is such that impromptu meetings spring up, it may not always be feasible to be on a conference call regularly. Face-time is premium in some cases. If you think about it, out of sight, out of mind really can come into play. Being present in the office is sometimes the best option.

2: The boss is a micromanaging jerk. Let's face it, if you work for a micromanager (and many people do), you'll probably never be allowed to take advantage of this perk. However, there may be ways around this. For example, if you're new enough with the company it may take some time to earn your boss' trust. Prove that you are a reliable employee. Over time, you will be allowed more leeway. If not, well, get used to seeing the walls of your cubicle. If your manager is the type that is nothing but insecure or a power freak, they will need to keep you under close watch at all times. It doesn't matter how good you are, these people will never bend. Remember, you are not in the business of managing or changing other people. You're in the business of managing and completing your own workload.

3: You are simply not reliable. You know if you are or not. Perhaps your boss is right to keep you in the office full-time. Are you a slacker? Do you spend more time surfing the Internet than you should be? Deep down, we know when we're working hard and when we're hardly working. You are simply not a good candidate for this and cannot be left on your own.

Keep in mind that I didn't enter office politics into this equation. That's a separate discussion and not a true black-or-white situation. I'm not saying that reason #2 is a good reason, but it's probably free from political motives (unless the boss keeps you around because they feel threatened by you). Of course, not everyone wants to work from home all the time either. There are many positive aspects to working in an office, such as having the company of others. Working alone at home can get lonesome.

Advice for the College Grad

To all graduating college seniors: congratulations! You're on your way to the start of what will hopefully be a lucrative career. Before you go anywhere, there are some things you need to know. Actually, there are A LOT of things to know, but most of them you'll figure out along the way.

Finding your first job may seem like the biggest challenge you face, but it isn't. In some cases, even though it may take months before you land your first gig, the real test comes during your first few months at the office. The most obvious piece of advice I could offer is lay low. Do your job well, but keep a low profile until you know the lay of the land. Use this time to learn how things operate in a corporate environment. Even then, **learning the job is just the basics**.

It's unfortunate, but you'll run into lousy people along the way and face many trials that test your sanity. Yes, I'm cynical... but I'm also being realistic. Sometimes it's not enough (nor is it okay) to use common sense; there will be others (possibly your boss) who will not do so. **Be prepared for this**.

Work is not like school. If you're the best in your class at school you can literally come out on top. Work is the polar opposite: You can be the best at what you do and be despised and punished for your acumen. **Tread carefully**.

Even when you know the lay of the land, the terrain can shift at a moment's notice. It's important to be flexible enough to roll with the punches. It's also important to know when you've had enough and need to bail. When you're young you can move around a bit to find that good fit. As long as you know that that "good fit" is rare.

The Boss Can Do No Wrong

People that have double standards are weak.

"Do as I say, not as I do" is bollocks. To be credible, you need to put your money where your mouth is. Employees that mimic your behavior are in a way trying to emulate you; good, bad, or indifferent. If you do something, people get the message that it's OK for them to do it too.

Apparently this isn't the case when it comes to gossip. I don't mean just office gossip, I mean office gossip about personal business. I knew a manager once who divulged secrets about another employee's personal life. Personal life, meaning - LIFE OUTSIDE OF THE OFFICE.

No good deed goes unpunished. This same manager caught wind of something said about *their* personal life. I don't know whether the gossip was true or not, but they had closed-door meetings with those suspected of spreading the gossip. I don't know whether those suspected were guilty or not, either. I just know that the employee originally gossiped about was rendered powerless against management's attacks.

It's interesting to note how it was okay for this person to mouth off about their employees, but they got all shocked and shaken when someone talked about them. Seems only right to me.

Hey, what comes 'round, goes 'round, no? Everyone gets a turn.

What's the point?

Office politics are like being back in high school: if you're in with the cool kids, you'll be fine. If you're not, then you'll live in fear of being beat down every day and suffering atomic wedgies from being uncool. With this one, you're either in or out. You either jump into the deep end or stay out. It's difficult to pull off being diplomatic, no matter how hard you try. It doesn't even matter that you do your job well or not. If you don't go along with the boss, your perceived performance goes down the proverbial tubes. Once that happens, there is very little chance of your career with the company ever resurrecting itself. Time to move on or get fired.

Lesson learned:

It's all about the ego and being part of the "in" crowd. Just like in high school, the rules of engagement change without notice. Be prepared. If you were golden one day, you'll be crap the next. It can literally change overnight. Interestingly, people will go as far as to make up stories about you, too. This was an email I received from Emily:

> "One of the stories that circulated about me was that my friend was writing my resume for me at his desk, during office hours. Let me just say: I would have to be stupid to A) Have someone else write my resume for me (since I'm a writer) and B) To work on my resume AT THE OFFICE!!! Come on."

Bottom line is, you need to be so careful with this one. It's a very fine line to walk. Once you're on the wrong side, there's just not much to be done other than transfer to a different department or a different company altogether.

CHAPTER NINE

Killing La Vida Loca

"I can't come in today because I'm in jail." - *Unknown*

How To: Call In Sick

The excuses are virtually limitless:

- I won't be in to work today because I've been tripping on Peyote for the last few days, and I can't seem to find my legs.
- The dog ate my car keys. We're going to hitchhike to the vet.
- My mother-in-law has come back as one of the Undead and we must track her to her coffin to drive a stake through her heart and give her eternal peace. One day should do it.

Per Careerbuilder.com's absenteeism survey late last year, **43%** of the workers said they called out sick in the last year when they weren't really sick. This number was up from **35%** the year before. The most popular day of the week to call in? *Wednesday*.

63% of the hiring managers stated that they were more suspicious of people calling in sick on Mondays or Fridays. (I'm guessing people know this if they're calling out on Wednesdays).

The results from Career Builder also said that **38%** of the people surveyed felt that sick days are equivalent to vacation days. Hmmm.

The most common reason for calling out sick when not sick was to *relax or catch up on things at home*. The others included going to a doctor's appointment, running errands or they just plain old didn't feel like going in.

Making the Call:

There's a right way and a wrong way to call in sick. For starters, you need to remember to call!

When you make the call remember to keep things as simple as possible. If you can, call early and leave voicemails. Avoiding a conversation minimizes the possibility of slipping up. Know what you're going to say before you pick up the phone.

The reason can be brief: "I don't feel well, so I'm not going to come in." It's simple and to the point. Don't elaborate too much on a reason. You have a bug, a headache, whatever. It doesn't need to be more detailed than that.

When you leave the message, be sure that the television or radio isn't blasting in the background. If there's noise in the background, this can reduce the efficacy of your excuse. If you're really sick, you're going to be in bed... play it up. Speak quietly or raspy or however you can to convey the image that you are unwell.

Be smart: don't come back to work the next day with a suntan if you've been at the beach. Nothing will cut your credibility faster than being caught like this! Let's see you weasel your way out of that one.

Also, try not to take off more than one day at a time if possible. Some employers want a doctor's note for two or more days missed. Know what your company's policies are ahead of time if you can.

So let me know when you call out so we can play hookey together!

Too Sick to Work?

We all know that there are plenty of people out there who have called in sick when they were OK to work.

There are many reasons for this:
- People need to take a "mental health" day.
- Something came up.
- There are too many chores that need to get done.

Lastly, and my favorite,

Your bat-$@#%-crazy manager drives you to do it. (Of course, this could go under "mental health" day, but I think it needs its own category).

Mental Health Day. People need to take a mental health day. This, more and more, is becoming widely acceptable as a reason for calling out. Mental stress is just as valid a reason as physical stress, to need time off to "defrag". Sometimes it just feels good to watch morning re-runs of "Little House on the Prairie" rather than deal with the joys of work. Believe me, I would have rather watched episodes of "Saved by the Bell" and/ or "Trading Spouses" than go in most days. Believe me; I would rather swallow razor blades than watch that kind of television on any other day. Besides, sometimes it is absolutely necessary to go to the beach in order to make oneself feel better.

Something Came Up. Of course personal days should be used in most cases for last-minute issues, but if you have the sick days to burn, then every so often this isn't a bad option. Are you having furniture delivered or is the cable guy coming by for an appointment? Are you really going to go to work after coming in at 4 am from seeing U2 and then driving half the night back home? How functional will you be at work? It shouldn't be a crime to take a sick day as long as it's done within reason.

Chores. Again, personal days should be used for things like this, but sometimes it can't be avoided. I mean, you can only take so many personal days when you're interviewing for other jobs.

The Devil Made Me Do It. Sometimes your manager is an idiot and you just cannot be around the stupidity for another minute. Constant exposure to that couldn't possibly be good for your health. Also, if this idiot has caused a ridiculous amount of stress, then you actually will be sick when you call out. I remember taking a sick day once to have an upper endoscopy performed to confirm acid reflux. It was something that I looked forward to because I would have the day off. There's something really wrong when you look forward to having a medical procedure like this done just to have a day off from work. But I was. Trust me, I wish I had twelve wisdom teeth, just so I could have time off for having each one extracted.

All in all, sick days need to be taken when you are truly sick. It's also important for employers to remember that happy employees don't call out sick as often as the unhappy ones. There's a correlation there to be aware of. If you find yourself calling out more and more when you're not actually sick, it may be time to ask yourself if it's time to move on.

Bullies Hurt Business

I mean really, you'd think that this was a no-brainer. However, I found this quote that says research shows how bullied employees are not engaged 100% in their work:

> "What the research has shown… is that employees of bullies withhold the extras, i.e. they are not fully engaged or giving 100 percent. For example, they may treat customers poorly, do average as opposed to excellent work and spend countless working hours complaining about the boss to their colleagues and friends. Clearly, the organization suffers in both tangible and intangible ways when managers push employees around."

Additionally, they treat others poorly and spend a lot of time commiserating with anyone who will listen. Aside from the fact that people need to research things that we don't already know, this is just ridiculous. It's ridiculous because WHAT DO YOU EXPECT? Who really expects positive results from bullying their employees?

I don't know about you, but when I'm called worthless and incompetent it makes me take pride in my company and what I do. Duh.

Is the Grass Greener?

By now, you've all heard me relate various mis-adventures in management. Come to think of it, many people have heard these stories. Of course, there's almost an unending supply of them.

A funny thing happened. Not funny "ha-ha", but funny in a "hmmm" kind of way. As I perused the many stories posted by other disillusioned workers across the country on various websites and blogs, I realized that working for idiot bosses and with idiot co-workers was actually the norm rather than the exception. I've seen this on message boards and read plenty of material that go on about micromanagement, bullies and your garden-variety idiot bosses.

So, looking back at my lengthy job search I have to wonder: Is the grass really greener on the other side?

Let's take a look at some of the places I've interviewed with. One place surprised me by conducting a panel interview – which was okay – except that the head interviewer was a pompous weasel. Overall, I got a weird vibe and was very uncomfortable. This was a position that was recommended to me. I should have realized something was up when the person who referred me warned me in advance about the head interviewer. Hmmm.

Then there was another similar position I interviewed for that I found out a colleague of mine got instead. Sure, I was disappointed initially, but I got over it. Thing is, when I met up with this former colleague shortly after he left, he seemed pretty unhappy with the new job and the way things were run in that organization. Another "hmmm".

Then the last one, the granddaddy of them all took a long

time to play itself out. I was referred to another company for yet another similar position and hit it off beautifully with the person who would be my potential boss. All signs pointed to me getting this job. He even told me flat-out that he wanted me for it. THEN, I met his boss and things started going downhill. His boss was let go and the position I was going for went with him. But, I hadn't given up hope because the gentleman I first interviewed with said that he may be able to convince the new management on the position. Okay. Then shortly thereafter I found out that this nice man was "let go" due to changes in management.

So really, who actually has it good in the workplace? Is there such a thing as having a "good" job? I would have to say that about 80% of the people I know in the workforce are unhappy with their work conditions. Who has a great boss? <Insert cricket sounds here> Is there any way to escape the office politics that so often dictate the overall environment of the company?

You know, I'm not so sure that it exists. When you look at it that way you really need to ask yourself: why is it so important to flee to another job in hopes of finding it "better"? The only two valid reasons I can come up with are:

1: Moving into a higher position for more money.

2: The current job that you're in is causing such mental and physical anguish that you truly need to leave out of fear for your health.

So, the urgency I felt to look for a new job eventually dissipated. There didn't seem to be much of a point once I made the decision to go solo. Even still, there just didn't seem to be anything out there that answered enough of my needs to make me happy day-in and day-out. At least I know what to expect working for myself. If I become disappointed in my standards, then it's completely up to me to do something about them. Given my abilities, I can adapt and make something work. It's difficult to leave that kind of happiness up to someone else. It doesn't exist there.

Every Second Counts

It's a given that employees are paid for working an agreed-upon amount of time. The work hours are typically established before one begins a new job.

It's a given as well that any time missed should be made up. If you come in a little late, stay a little late after hours. You guys know the drill. Do your best to be at work on time and work the allotted time. It also shows some amount of respect for your co-workers who show up and work when expected.

Now on the other hand, this monitoring of time can get out of hand very easily. If, for instance, your supervisor is the micromanager from hell it will already be out of control.

You can only do your best with these people. Your (micro)manager's ways are theirs, not yours. Don't get nuts over it.

Be smart about your work time– do what you're hired to do and give it everything you can.

Your Life or Your Career?

It's a fairly standard notion that starting out in any professional career means having to pay your dues in order to move up the ladder. But how high are those dues now?

After working for twelve years in my industry, I ended up working longer hours (and consistently so) than ever before. It goes without saying that you need to be willing and flexible when you set your sights on that nice promotion. Even still, if there's no promotion in your immediate future, it would probably help to work a little extra here and there. Maybe volunteer for a new project in addition to your daily workload.

But, it gets to a point where you need to stop and ask yourself what you're really doing it for. In my situation – and I hardly think I'm alone on this one – I've gone almost six whole years without a promotion and yet my hours got longer and longer and steadily so for a good chunk of that time.

So I took a look at my situation and asked myself what I was doing. Interestingly, I had no good answer. I was wasting what I saw as valuable time – as well as my partying years.

Partying aside, I had no life during the work week. Just what would I have done if I had a family? I realized that I was losing time to do things for myself that I wanted to do. It wasn't the life that I envisioned for myself.

I wasn't a doctor or a lawyer or an investment banker where the money was rolling in. I was just an average Jane, working for a decent salary, though I was far from wealthy.

So folks, I'm more or less throwing this question out into the cosmos; Why do we have to do this? How many out there are happy slaving at the offices for ridiculous amounts of time that they will probably never get back?

I once heard something that I thought was interesting. I wish I could remember now where it was that I heard it. Back in the earlier part of the 20th century, people speculated that due to all of the technological advances taking place, it would cut production time/work time into a fraction of what it was then (and they were basing that on an 8-hour work day). They said that in another 80 years or something people would only have a 2-hour workday (or something silly like that). So why is it that with all of these wonderful advances we're working longer and harder rather than smarter?

Just something I'm tossing out there.

The Age of IM

In an age of email, cell phones, Blackberrys and Instant Messaging, staying connected is paramount, particularly in business.

But let's just talk about Instant Messaging. IM is one of those neat little technological advances that helps keep people in touch with one another. When merely calling someone on the phone isn't quick enough, one can count on IM. It's easy enough to access, you can respond at your leisure, and it's easy to end the conversations.

Many people and businesses rely heavily on it. Of course, not everyone needs it. Many times it's an easy way to say "Hi" to a friend during the work day without the interruption of a phone call. It's easy to use IM during business hours and makes it appear as though you're working. But that's neither here nor there.

The long and short of it is that everyone's using it. While during the work day personal use should be kept to a minimum, it does help to get work done.

What I found interesting was that where I used to work, IM was frowned upon. While everyone else in the company used it as much as email, we poor schlubs got the beat-down for being caught on it. As a matter of fact, one of our job goals was to be "mindful of the fact that Instant Messaging... be used only during pre-work, lunch or post-work hours." Yeah.

Then the company goes and rolls out its own intra-office IM. What's interesting about that is that those in power used it probably more than the rest of us. Hmmm...

So is IM the enemy or were the powers-that-be just looking to wield their might over those beneath them? I don't get it.

(Yet) Another Bad Boss Story

Dear Gail,

My boss is a negative guy... but when I say Negative, I really mean Negative and Malignant. For instance, one day he calls the I.R.-FREAKING-S. (yes, those guys who steal all that money from your paycheck). A woman answers the phone with what is clearly an African-American dialect. He asks for a specific department. The woman asks for his identifying information before transferring him, to log the call. He replies out of the blue, "Ma'am, I don't need your black attitude" and hangs up.

Separate incident: Boss announces to me a week before Thanksgiving that I'm leaving for Taiwan to baby sit *his* customer (Note: I don't make any commission of this project, but he'll make a $40,000 profit from it next year), on December 3. I'm in Taiwan from the 3rd to the 7th.

While I'm on this trip, he bitches at me that I need to make travel plans for the following week to "start seeing some customers". He also tells me that I'm going to Bulgaria, Turkey and Romania at the end of February.

Now, courtesy to someone who is currently babysitting your customer might be to split the commission in some fashion, or to at least wait until he returns to the U.S. before pushing him into another exhausting week of international travel. Not from Skippy the Dumb***.

So, to recap: Week of 11/28 - 12/2, I'm in Michigan and Ohio for three days. Get back Thursday night, spend Friday in the office. Fly out on Saturday, baby sit his customer for a week and fly back the following Saturday. Get to the office for Monday and Tuesday, fly to Chicago for a trip Wednesday through Friday. Then, I STILL get the, "You-need-to-be-on-the-road-more-meeting-customers-otherwise-you'll-never-make-any-money" routine.

As the Cynical Employee, I said, "Hmmm... don't you think if I wasn't wasting a week babysitting your customer and NOT making any money on that, might bear an opportunity cost that keeps me from meeting new customers and growing my business?"

Oh, and I get treated like a cheap whore of a secretary at the same time. While he's sitting on the phone chatting with his buddies about town politics, an email will come in from his second largest customer. He'll then tell me, "Cynical Employee, forward that email to this guy, this guy, this guy and this guy. Then enter it in the quote log." (Incidentally, he doesn't even know how to use the quote log, so I generally skip that step.)

So when Cynical Employee finds a new job, his boss will consider it the ultimate betrayal.

Anyway, that's C.E.'s thoughts. Talk to you later, good luck sticking it to the Man.

-Cynical Employee

<u>Once Upon a Root Canal</u>

Once upon a time (but not so long ago that the painful memory was erased), I had the unfortunate experience of my first – and hopefully last - root canal procedure. All in all, I have to say it wasn't so bad. I mean, when you had to work every day with what I had to work with, suddenly root canal didn't look so ugly.

So I did what I had to do and dealt with it. My dental appointments were scheduled during lunch hours. That said, I had to go back one time to be fitted for a crown. As I mentioned, this was my first root canal so I didn't really know what I was getting into, right?

This one particular appointment was set for 2p.m., which was later than the time I normally took for lunch. I cleared it with The Supreme Micromanager a day in advance and explained what I was having done. Okay.

The next day, I reminded my boss about the late lunch hour and the dental appointment. She said "Okay".

Long story short, my appointment ran well over the 1-hour time I allotted for it. But what am I supposed to do? I can't exactly call the boss and say I'll be late - half my head is numb, and I have dental paraphernalia protruding from my mouth – not exactly the right time for conversation.

It ran 45 minutes over.

I got back to the office with a wretched headache from the drilling and stabbing hunger pangs since I hadn't had the chance to eat before the appointment. When I stopped by my boss's office to say that I was back, she looked at me with the stoniest expression I'd ever seen on anyone.

"Where were you?"

Huh? "I was at the dentist, just as I told you."

"You were gone a long time. I had no idea what happened to you."

Mom? Is that you? Am I fifteen again? Did the dentist

administer something other than straight-up Novocain? As if the root canal wasn't enough damage for one day, I had to take this abuse from my bat-#$@% crazy manager.

"Uh... (Checking to be sure no saliva ran out of the corner of my very numb mouth), I told you that I was going to the dentist. He had to fit me for a crown. It took longer than we thought and I couldn't call you. Sorry."

"Well, I want to know how you're going to make the time up."

Ugh.

"I'll work through lunch tomorrow. Again, I'm sorry."

Yeah, I was sorry that the procedure was over and that I had to go back to the office. Having root canal was more fun than being in my job. Actually, I take that back... I can handle the job. So let's just say that the crown fitting was more fun than this encounter after the appointment.

I'm sorry that she hates me and walks all over my self esteem every other day. I'm sorry for whatever it was I did in a past life that landed me in this god-awful spot. I'm sorry that I have to suffer the daily abuse and wonder if today will be my last day at the job - and in an industry I've worked in for so long.

I'm really sorry that in two years' time I was unable to find suitable employment elsewhere to get away from the self esteem stealer and heal my wounds.

Believe it or not, I really do try my best not to wallow in self pity.

I'm *not* sorry however, that enduring this garbage every day for far too long has forced me to take hold of my future and start my own business. If I can work this hard for someone else and handle that nonsense, think of what I can do for myself.

When I told my friend this story, she had this to say: "What you probably should have done was, while you had seventeen apparatuses in your mouth, you should have signaled to the nurse by "blinking" out your sentence. You should have said, would you please call my boss and tell her I will be longer than expected. Keep the bloody cotton balls from your mouth. Then when you go back you can pelt her with them! She really sounds like she is too stupid to live."

Yet another friend of mine chimed in with: "Morse code… or maybe you should have tried sending up smoke signals."

I just don't get it. My own mother didn't even treat me that way when I was a child. How about asking if I was okay for starters? Then you can politely remind me that I need to make up whatever time I owe.

A Hard Day's Work?

Hardly. Why some people move up remains a mystery. There are those that work hard and those that succeed. The following is a story from my friend Georgia, who had such an experience:

"A few months ago, I had a "discussion" with my moron manager about the importance of "working smart".

She went on and on about how important it was to put in a lot of overtime. As if this would be my free pass to getting a promotion. As part of her loony diatribe that working lots of overtime = super stardom, The Moron mentioned a fellow manager as a positive example. She went on to say that "Miss Treat" was seen working at all hours in the office.

I almost fell off my chair.

Yeah, Miss Treat may have been seen at all hours in the office, but I'd hardly say that she was working that whole time. Or even a lot of it. Maybe none of it.

You see, I used to sit right next to Miss Treat. And OHHHHH what a "treat" she used to be!

When The Moron said her name I was shocked. I said, "You mean she actually takes time out from doing her nails to get work done? I thought that was why she had minions, uh, I mean assistants."

The Moron looked at me all confused. Uh, hello? I reminded her, "You and I used to have conversations about The Perpetual Manicure. I used to escape to your office *because the smell of the nail polish fumes used to smoke me away from my desk!!!*"

Now The Moron is using Miss Mani/Pedi as a ROLE MODEL for work??? I'd like to say that she was kidding, but she wasn't smiling. I know I shouldn't be surprised when I talk to her – ever – but I just couldn't help it. This was one of those times. I just couldn't believe what she was telling me.

What I really wanted to come back at her with was, "Well, if your idea of working hard is giving yourself a manicure, then hell... I'll do that *and then* I'll give myself a pedicure!" I'll show YOU how dedicated I am! (Though of course, it won't be pretty for anyone when I rub my heels with a pumice stone).

This is the kind of "advice" she gives me. Thank you so much. How did I ever get this far in my life without her?"

Will You Please Keep It Down?

Tell me something: Why is it okay for the "upper echelon" of the office to have an ongoing "coffee break" that's disruptive to others, yet the rest of us schmoes get dirty looks when we stop to say "Good Morning" to a colleague?

It's irritating, it's rude, and it's obnoxious. Why is it so hard for them to keep their voices down when socializing in their offices? Why should I have to not only listen to what's going on, but lose my concentration because they're shrieking with laughter? No joke... they sound like a bunch of banshees.

I just want to shout at them: **"SHUT THE HELL UP OR SHUT YOUR DOOR. YOU SOUND LIKE MONKEYS ON CRACK. THE REST OF US ARE ACTUALLY TRYING TO GET WORK DONE!!!"**

You know, I don't think I'd even mind it so much if they actually fostered a friendly and warm environment. But they don't. They don't encourage any socialization amongst the workers. You begin to feel guilty for having social conversations and start to look over your shoulder at every turn.

Why is it this way? Why don't employers realize that happy employees work harder? They're more willing to go the extra mile. That, in turn, equals a larger bottom-line for the company. This isn't me just blowing steam. There are studies that prove this: companies could be earning HUNDREDS OF MILLIONS OF DOLLARS MORE by improving employee morale.

After the Root Canal...

So when I had to have my root canal, I scheduled all the appointments during my lunch hour and returned to the office afterward. What a mistake that was. Aside from being reamed out by my manager when I returned a little late from my appointments (that she knew about in advance and which I made all my time up from), there was one occasion where I was marched straight into a meeting with a VP in the sales department.

The reason for the meeting was to settle the particulars of an account. In order for my department to do their job, we needed certain information. With bureaucratic red tape what it is, it was not a simple matter to settle, nor was it one that anyone wanted to own.

So, enter me and my manager. We met with this VP and a few members of his staff.

We arrived at the VP's office before his staff did. My boss dove headstrong into her loony diatribe when the VP asked her to wait until the others joined us. She heard it, but didn't acknowledge it. She continued right on until the VP told her for a second time to wait. So right there we were off to a great start.

Once everyone else got there and things picked right back up, I was further mortified by her behavior. It wasn't overtly brutal or nasty... but in her deluded way of trying to drive the point home, she really hit them over the head – as though she was speaking to a group of children. They knew what she was getting at – anyone would have "gotten" it. But for some reason, she wouldn't lay off and eventually the VP cut the meeting short and escorted us out.

I never said a word during that meeting (I was still in too much pain from the root canal). But after we left, my manager commented how curt she thought the VP became toward us. My head was spinning but I knew what went on in there. How did she not see it? She was impolite and demanding - and that's putting it politely. No wonder we were escorted out. There are better ways to approach others for what you want. She should learn them.

Welcome to the Toolbox

Some of the issues people have at work is influenced by coworkers. A supervisor may be quick to believe another employee before their own. As hard as that may seem to hear, it can be quite true. Regina told me how she was thrown under the bus when a lying coworker got her into some hot water:

"One of the reasons I was placed in hell (other than drawing the unlucky short-stick for two years), is because someone failed to do their job which put me in the direct line of fire with my supervisor.

In order for me and my team to complete the project at hand, we needed information from a Third Party individual who also works in my department. This Third Party supplied us with incorrect information **three times** and then proceeded to **lie about it** to my boss to cover their ass.

Isn't that delightful?

This didn't go over very well with my bat-$#@%-crazy manager. Even though the Third Party person was blatantly **wrong**, it fueled the doubts already in my manager's mind about me.

Then, as I went to my idiot boss to tell her – for the third time – that the information given to us was incorrect, she mentioned that she spoke to *her* manager about it. Apparently, whatever we saw as *"incorrect"* on the report wasn't in fact *"wrong"*. Oh really?

When we received it we were told that it was the "final" version. So, when "Point A" is actually *supposed to be* "Point B", it's **NOT** wrong? When I asked my manager this, she only shrugged her shoulders. That's just great.

What I'd like to know is, why are they protecting the Third Party so much? How did they get to be the pet?

What's even nicer is that I was passed over for a promotion by this bright and shining Third Party the year before. It's nice to see how hard work, dedication and having half a brain pay off."

It is generally expected that subordinates will be protected by their supervisors. Good, bad or indifferent... part of the "team" mentality is that someone has your back. This is the way it ought to be – in theory.

Your Job is Doomed

"Just because I'm paranoid doesn't mean that they aren't out to get me." - *Woody Allen*

Does the following mean I'm out?

This is a list, not all-inclusive, that tells you you're on your way out of a job:

- Your boss, mentor, or champion leaves or is suddenly rendered powerless.
- You fail to meet expectations or are a poor performer.
- You are on progressive discipline (verbal or written warning).
- You find yourself increasingly out of the loop.
- You are given a less desirable or lucrative territory.
- Your compensation structure changes dramatically.
- You are watched and micromanaged where you once had freedom.
- You are given new, unattainable goals or targets.
- You get a new boss who comes from the outside.
- You are in an underperforming unit.
- You are in a nonrevenue- producing or overstaffed unit.
- You are in a remote office.
- You have the least tenure or were the last one hired.
- You have a significant salary.
- You are no longer included in future plans or upcoming projects.
- You are passed over for a promotion.
- You fail to accept a position or relocation.
- Your opinion is now worthless.
- You are reassigned to a lower- profile project.
- You are demoted.
- You are given a "take it or leave it" or "no win" option.
- Management makes your life a living hell.

The following further details the signs that you're being pushed out:

You find yourself increasingly out of the loop

If you find yourself shut out of meetings and the last to know what's going on, the company may be preparing for life without you. I had this very thing happen to me and then I was lied to about it. Nice.

You are passed over for a promotion.

I worked for five years in a pioneering role within my department. When a promotion did become available, it went to someone who was new with the company and had no experience in that particular role. You can imagine how that made me feel.

You are demoted / You are in an underperforming unit / You are reassigned to a lower- profile project.

Instead of getting a promotion, I was involuntarily moved into a different, less desirable role. The position I had been in offered high visibility where this new role gave me none. On top of that, I was placed in charge of under-performing individuals.

You are watched and micromanaged where you once had freedom.

To quote Kate Lorenz at Careerbuilder.com, "If you have always had a great deal of autonomy in the past and are now being scrutinized at every turn, there might be a serious reason behind this new form of management. Whether you feel you need your hand held or not, new scrutiny in the workplace can sometimes mean less confidence in your abilities." What I don't understand is, after all this time, why is it my management still refuses to provide examples of where I fall short? I'm not entirely sure that this means lack of confidence in my abilities or if it's just that they want me out.

You have received one or more negative reviews.

Once again per Kate, "If you have multiple bad reviews under your belt and still haven't learned from them, your days probably are numbered. Just as bad, if you've had stellar reviews in the past and suddenly you are no longer regarded as a star performer, watch out!" It's true, if you have received a poor performance review you need to find out why. If your supervisor lays out a map of where you went wrong and what you can do to improve, then it's in your best interest to sit up and take notice. On the other hand, if your supervisor fails to provide this information then that too sends a strong message. So definitely "watch out" if this is happening to you – your company may be setting you up for involuntary departure.

You are on progressive discipline (verbal or written warning). As with your performance review, if your manager provided you with a solid outline of where you've fallen short, pay attention. Are these valid points? If they are, then do what you need to in order to stay employed - if that's what you want. If not, take this as a sign that they want you out. You can try to take your case to human resources if you think they'll listen. But be careful as they may side with your boss (and it's likely they will). Personally, I think it's better to stand up and fail then to do nothing. If it fails though, then it might be time to re-think your job and start looking elsewhere for employment. Trust me on this one – it's not a good sign.

If you truly feel you're being pushed out of your job then the best solution is to probably leave. It's unfair, but that doesn't mean you should stay and prove them wrong. Chances are, you'll lose.

What do YOU want to do? I don't know, what do YOU want to do?

I recently perused through Monster.com's message boards and read a few posts that were related to workplace bullying. Let me tell you, there's all kinds of people unleashed on this world... it's a little scary.

There were posts by individuals telling their tales of

being bullied, and in the process, they sounded as though they themselves could be accused of bullying. People are wacky sons-of-guns.

One person posted a message on the topic of missing deadlines. They said that it's unfair to say that a boss is bullying you if they are expecting work to be done on-time. "Don't miss deadlines because you can't get everything done… work with your boss to prioritize not only your tasks but your time."

They go on to say that leaving work before your work is done because you've been there all day is probably not viewed favorably. Keep your boss in the loop on the status of your work and it will go a long way in showing how hard you work and what exactly you're accomplishing. Don't assume they know – as they've got their own jobs to worry about.

I have a few things to say about this. First of all, they didn't know the people I worked for. I could not make a move (even to the restroom) without the loons knowing about it. Every day I provided updates on the projects that were on my desk. In between all the expected work, they dropped new projects and ad hoc requests on my lap. They did this and expected the other work to be done at the same time – and according to the original deadlines.

It eluded me as to how I could get it all done within the same timeframe. I mean, if there's a new project that arises, I should be allowed to have the time to work on it.

On countless occasions, I'd asked which project was priority. And then I'd get The Answer: "It's all priority. It all needs to be done."

Really? I was actually thinking I could throw something out or sweep it under the carpet.

But my immediate manager said it as though it was the dumbest question she'd ever heard. As if I should have known which was most important. Um, no… if there's unexpected projects that crop up, I can't know which is more important than the other if you don't say so! Especially since my luck is usually that if I hand one project in, she'll have wanted the other... and so forth.

Then I get the "You need to learn how to prioritize your responsibilities." Like I'm an idiot. I've been in this business for a long time, don't patronize me. When I press for an answer on what is MOST important she continues to respond with, "It's all important and it all needs to be done."

"Ok, but which do you want first?" I ask.

"I want it all done... it all needs to be done." Again, as if that answers everything.

"I understand that, but which do you need on your desk completed first?" At which she shakes her head and gets annoyed. So I continue, "I can only work on one thing at a time... which would you like me to work on first?"

There, that was the wrong thing to say.

"If you can only work on one thing at a time then you need to learn how to multi-task."

Um, no... this isn't like preparing Thanksgiving dinner when you calculate how long to cook the turkey and then to cook the potatoes, steam the string beans, etc. so that it's all on the table at the same time. THIS IS BUSINESS – it works differently.

Bottom line, I got no direction from her, and regardless of what my game plan was, it was never good enough.

It was usually at that point that I would realize (yet again) there's no winning and the only obvious solution was to 1: Work through lunch, 2: Work late, 3: Bring work home and 4: Work on the weekends – in order to get it all done.

So in theory, yes – it makes all the sense in the world to work on a schedule with your manager and keep them in the loop. It's a good idea. It was just another thing that did not work for me. I'll continue to take that advice, but I will also continue to get beat up for it.

And that's all I have to say about that.

This is a No-Win Situation

Once the normal methods have been tried - unsuccessfully

- to get through to another human being, it helps to know when to quit. My friend A.J. was going through a rough time at her job right around the same time that I was. Her stories used to kill me; I mean, I thought I had it bad!

This was one of her stories:

"It's Friday evening at 5:55pm and I'm about to leave for the weekend. Against my better instincts, I answered a call from my manager. She asked me to stop by before I left. Okay.

When I stepped into her office she said to me, "I know you don't want to hear it, but I need to know where you're at with your quarterly report."

What an interesting way to start a conversation. And I don't mean interesting-good. It's true, she did know that this report had been a thorn in my side but that was due to situations beyond my control. As per Murphy's law, if it could go wrong it would - and it did, which I was being blamed for. Of course, even if a meteor demolished the city block where our office was, I'd be blamed for not getting the report completed. She wouldn't want to hear it that the office no longer existed along with the rest of Manhattan's East Side.

"That's not true. I don't mind 'hearing it' about this report, and I don't mind discussing it. As my manager you're entitled to ask me about it. So let's talk about it."

"I need to know where you're at with it. As you're aware, this report was due on Wednesday. When can I expect it to be completed?"

Perfectly valid question.

I shrugged my shoulders, "I'm not sure".

Not what she wanted to hear but it was an honest response. She looked exasperated. "Why not? You knew in advance when this report was due. Why didn't you plan better to get it done?"

Hmmm, let's see...

To begin with: starting the report was dependent upon receiving quarterly information, which only became available three weeks ago. If I don't have the data, I can't work on the report. With me so far?

I'm currently short-handed; down one assistant. On the same day that this information became available to us to start work, my second assistant put in their two-week notice. Management decided to keep Assistant #2 since I was already short-handed. So, aside from the fact that I'd already been covering my managerial responsibilities and the first assistant's responsibilities, I then had to pick up the responsibilities of the second. That meant I had to carry the workload of three people. I don't need to tell you that a person who hands in their notice is a lame duck. But on the day our data came in, I began working on the project and I asked Assistant #2 to please work on it as well (I told them, "You're not being escorted out the door so you may as well do something while you're here"). As you can imagine, I should be grateful that Assistant #2 did any work at all on it.

Every day I checked in with her to give a status report on what was completed and what had yet to be done. In her universe, this was all okay.

That was two weeks prior to Christmas. Now, I happen to work quickly on this particular project but the fact remains that there's still the day-to-day workload of three people to handle. So I'm handling that workload, plus working on this, in the meantime. On top of that, I had three vacation days that I needed to take (or else I'd lose them). These were all approved with full knowledge of the current workload.

Additionally, prior to taking the three days off before Christmas, I confirmed my new hire's training schedule with the company's training group. My new assistant (scheduled to start work on the first Monday after Christmas) was slated to be in training ALL DAY Monday, Tuesday and partially on Wednesday. That meant that I would have Monday, Tuesday and half of Wednesday to work on this other project – and potentially get it done.

Ha!

What actually happened: The internal training group completely changed the training schedule so I had to train the new employee ALL DAY Monday, half day Tuesday, and half day Thursday. But of course I had no prior knowledge of this as I don't check emails on my vacations. Why should I? I'm trying to enjoy my time off, you know?

My manager knew all of this and did nothing.

On top of that, my manager – who is my back-up – didn't back me up on ANYTHING while I was out. It took me four days to catch up on all the nonsense that went on in my absence that she did nothing about. In that three day time span, I also received over six hundred emails.

So when was this report supposed to get done? I didn't even glance at it when I came back - it was not physically possible. She knew about all of this.

I explained to her about the six hundred emails, piles of report requests (that were not handled in my absence), the training schedule and daily workload of three people that I was carrying. None of that mattered.

"But you knew ahead of time and you should have anticipated that obstacles would come up."

No - I could not have anticipated that I would have over six hundred emails in my inbox when I returned.

I could not (but should) have anticipated that she would not have lifted a finger to help me – after she said she would (and as my back up she's supposed to, right? At least a little bit).

I could not have anticipated that the company's training group would have totally altered the agreed-upon schedule for my new employee.

These were obstacles that could not have been anticipated.

I could however, anticipate crushing her head between my thumb and index finger as I squinted at her from the opposite end of the room.

"Well you know, we have a problem then," I said. "Although I'm telling you on a daily basis everything that goes down and how I'm handling them, you don't tell me until it's too late that it's not okay." I took a deep breath, "You have expectations that I don't seem to be living up to. So let me ask you, what should I have done instead of doing what I did?"

A smirk swept across her face. I anticipated choking her with steel wool to wipe it off.

"Seriously, I want to be able to do things your way – but you need to share with me what that way is. If you have any suggestions as to how I could have handled this better, then please share them with me... I want to be able to work better with you. Let's discuss this so that you have no further disappointments in the future."

In return for that nice little comment I received nothing but a blank stare. She said nothing. Nothing. I have thought of every last way to get through to this woman and they have all failed.

Folks trust me – if you've reached this point with your managers and hit nothing but brick wall after brick wall... then it's time to cut your losses and find employment elsewhere. Find a job where your input and performance are valued. Nobody should have to endure abuse like this."

When I shared A.J.'s story with my other friends they had this to say:

"Seriously... get the hell out of there before someone gets hurt." And: "You'd have a decent case- "temporary insanity"- if she turns up missing! Time to speed up the end-game!"

Nice.

Does Having a "Good" Attitude Pay Off?

This is yet another article that I read that I had to add my two cents to. In this piece provided by Careerbuilder.com, your attitude, and *not* your brains, take you places. The following are ten attitudes that will help propel your career (of course I had to put my two cents in here too; in a concise and cynical, though upbeat, style):

1. I am in charge of my destiny.

I got news for you... you're really not.

2. Anything is possible.

Yes. Anything IS possible. Do not think that you will be rewarded one day and not thrashed the next – regardless of the amazing work you've done or if you've invented the wheel. Your career can go rapidly down the tubes with no warning.

3. No task is too small to do well.

Actually, it IS if you've been thrown a few steps back in your career. You can find yourself doing work that you'd done years ago.

4. Everyone is a potential key contact.

Beware: they can also be a potential key threat.

5. I was made to do this job... and the one above me.

Please – I was made to do this job and YOURS, boss.

6. It's not just what I know, but who I know.

This is certainly true. It's always good to forge strong alliances along the way. That way when you need to bail (or you get tossed on your arse), you can call on them for help.

7. What else can I do?

It doesn't matter what you do. If you're liked, you'll succeed. If you're not, you can forget it. And oh yeah - you better make sure your parachute opens because when you do fall, you fall fast!

8. Failure will help pave the way to my success.

That sounds nice in theory. No, I take that back. My failures have paved the way to my new business. No more will I have to answer to a bat-$#%@-crazy manager.

9. I am my own biggest fan.

I should be… in tough times I'm my ONLY fan.

10. My opportunity monitor is never turned off.

You might not be able to do anything about those opportunities, but you can sure watch as others grab onto them and soar in their careers.

Wow, I sound bitter. Perhaps I am, but my experiences made me realize that all the good sense in the world will do nothing if those you report to have none. So, is this bad stuff? Maybe. But then again, if it weren't for these experiences, I would never have been placed on my current path… which I love.

Compulsively Stupid

That's my idiot manager in a nutshell.

In a book titled *Coping with Toxic Managers, Subordinates… and Other Difficult People* by Dr. Roy H. Lubit, he describes the core characteristics of an obsessive-compulsive personality as:

1 – **Excessive focus on details and rules that interferes with the real objective.**
2 – **Rigid insistence that his or her own way should be followed.**
3 – **Difficulty with spontaneity and warm emotions.**
4 – **Exaggerated focus on work and achievement.**
5 – **Indecisiveness.**

Ladies and Gentlemen, I think we have a winner!!! This describes my bat-$#@%-crazy manager, how about yours?

Dr. Lubit also says that: "*...managers with compulsive personalities both micromanage and fail to provide the support subordinates need to perform at their best... The atmosphere these managers create is stifling.*"

"*Compulsive individuals excessively focus on details and are unable to see the big picture. They are also weak at knowing which details are important and which are not.*"

He goes on to say that once you get on the bad side of a compulsive individual, it's very difficult to redeem yourself (don't I know it!).

The problem that I have with the doctor's analysis is not how he describes this type of manager, but the way he explains **how to deal** with these people.

Dr. Lubit: Be responsive to their values and fears by phrasing things in ways they understand and can relate to. Stress punctuality with work. Indicate how important the work is, not whether or not you like it.

Here's something for them to respond to: YOU ARE IN THE WAY OF ME DOING MY JOB!!! I can't stress meeting deadlines as you like so much since you seek to sabotage my team meeting any of them. I can completely fake it about it being important since you already know that I hate it – thanks to you.

Dr. Lubit: Since they have limited trust in others, you need to fill them in on the details of what you are doing. The micromanagement might seem silly, but it's better to go along with it.

No – they need to learn how to function in mainstream society. I shouldn't have to change what's "normal" to fit in with that idiocy. It may be better to "go along with it", but you will be miserable! True, you cannot change your manager, but you don't have to stay there either.

Dr. Lubit: Compulsive managers prefer information in written format.

Please don't remind me of this one! Written documentation may be a good way to go, but these people love email SO much that they will bury you in it. They will want an answer for everything, but then they'll wonder why your work isn't complete since you apparently had the time to respond to thirty-one of their emails.

Dr. Lubit: Follow rules to the letter: Never come in late or leave early. Never complain about staying late. Never say that you want to spend time relaxing or having fun.

Yeah – because that sounds like something to look forward to every day. PLEASE sign me up for that job!!! Just one thing... you forgot to tell me to check my humanity at the door because apparently you're not allowed to have any working for these kinds of people.

Verbal Self-Defense

Well, you've heard me blab on about everyone's bad managers. It's important however, to expose this behavior for what it is: **Abusive**.

Abusive behavior in the workplace can take many forms. It can be outright physically violent and threatening, or it can be more subtle in the form of overly critical statements and negative comments about work performance or character traits.

Let's look at verbal abuse: *What is it?* It is language that:

Controls
Manipulates
Demeans

It attacks on the personal level – not on the issue.
Are you being verbally attacked? If you step out of a meeting

with your boss/co-worker and feel that you've been zinged, chances are you have been.

Watch for these signs:

-Does your boss/co-worker cut you down at every opportunity whether in public or private?
-Do you get baited?
-Are your best efforts met with destructive criticism?

Whether founded or unfounded, verbal abuse is counter-productive!

If you're being verbally attacked be careful:

-Respond, do *not* react
-Avoid "negative" language
-Find the positives
-Be alert and
-Stick to the issue at hand

It's important not to go off on a tangent – or allow the abuser to do so. It will be easier to cut that individual off or debunk their argument if you refuse to go on their little trip.

Be cool and breathe. You cannot be responsible for abusive individuals or the things that they will do or say. But you are in charge of your own reaction. Do not allow them to derail you.

Call a time-out for yourself: Sometimes things seem clearer once the dust settles.

Reconvene the meeting with the abusive individual if that's possible.

Again – *stick to the issue*!

It's also important to remember that you are not at fault and you're not crazy. I have gone through this and believe me, I know how ugly this can be.

Try to hang in there.

Guerilla Warfare in the Office

I get a real kick out of reading some of the business books that are currently available. I've said it before, I spend a great deal of time reading a lot of books that are out there to see if I've overlooked any possible solutions to my situation. By "solution" I mean a way to make it bearable for myself while I look for another job or start my own company. So far I've come up pretty empty. I get some laughs however, when I read some of this stuff. I'd like to share some of these gems with you.

Here's something I picked up from CNN/Money.com:

"If your boss is an unreasonable manager that overloads you with work, ask him what his priorities are and for options to deal with what you can't handle. Maybe even ask for a part-timer's help."

Okay. My experience makes me recall the attitude I'd get when I asked about the priorities - as if I should know which is more important to my boss. I'm not a mind-reader; if you don't tell me I won't know! As for asking for a part-timer's help, I'm going to refer to my favorite answer: "work through lunch, work late, bring work home and work on the weekends". And oh yeah, don't forget to take part in the ritual blood sacrifice required for the boss' amusement.

Here's another "tip": *The smart way to make promises is to be vague when possible. When your boss asks when you will finish a project, do not say exactly when. Be vague. For example, respond with, "I expect to have it done by the middle-to-latter part of the week." If that makes him happy, fine. If he wants more precision, however, you can always say: "I'm shooting for Wednesday afternoon."*

That's a nice try, but most of us live in the real world... most of the time. If I were to try this with my manager, she would get annoyed and ask which it was going to be – later this week or

Wednesday afternoon? So now if I say it's later this week and she doesn't like that and I then up it to Wednesday, I had better be darn sure that I have it ready for Wednesday. Then of course I have to be prepared for her to throw every obstacle in my path so that I cannot meet the Wednesday deadline. That'll play right into her belief that anything I say can't be believed and that she's right not to trust me. Remember that wire hanger scene from Mommy Dearest? That's how I used to feel emotionally. How could I be so stupid? Yeah, I wouldn't recommend this tactic. You REALLY need to know your boss before you pull any kind of "stunt". I'm not joking. It'll be easier for you that way.

Regularly document all contributions that you make to the company. Indicate the date, benefit to the company and benefit to the boss.

This is something that I've heard time and again. In some instances, this may be a good idea. However, it's also one of those things that can be very tricky – regardless of how well you handle it or how right you may be. I tried this very same tactic to defend myself in a follow-up meeting to a less-than-stellar review I once received. It didn't work. I recounted my contributions and the benefits to the company and to the boss. Lots of things went down at this particular time, which was when my manager also got promoted.

So, I listed all the positive things that I contributed - which I'm sure helped her to get that nice new title. I mean, if I was such a horrible employee, wouldn't that reflect negatively on her? Seriously, during a spell when I had weak people reporting to me I was hearing it left and right from management (insert finger-wagging here for emphasis) – none of it was good and they certainly didn't promote me. Long story short, when I tried this tactic I was written up. She probably felt exposed and undermined - which to be honest, when all was said and done, was what I wanted. It's too bad no one listened to me. My advice: *Be very careful with this one.*

Dr. Suzette Haden Elgin comments from her book *The Gentle Art of Verbal Self-Defense At Work*: "Any words, be they ever so flawless, can have their meaning cancelled by body language – but not vice versa. There are no words capable of cancelling the meaning transmitted by body language."

This one I just threw in for fun. There will be no need for words when you dive across their desk and start ripping the hair out of their head. What does that kind of body language say to you?

Someone once pointed out to me that, "Ironic that the same class of people who guerrilla warfare is usually used as a tactic to overthrow is attempting to utilize its principles." To which I responded, "Why go to a gun battle with snowballs? Fight fire with fire." I mean, honestly.

It's NOT my call!!!

The end of the year holidays are typically a busy time at work. People are usually trying desperately to clear their desks of work as they anticipate days off as well as preparing for the new year. Gabriel tells his story of what happened around the Thanksgiving holiday at his job:

"Two weeks before the Thanksgiving holiday I sat in my manager's office to "touch base" on current issues.

Issue #1: Vacation Time

Since the beginning of this year, I scheduled myself to take the two days off before Thanksgiving. That meant I was out Tuesday and Wednesday, but had to come in on Monday. This was okay with me – after all, I chose those days.

Now that the year was winding down, my manager told me that I had one more vacation day to schedule. He needed to know when I wanted to take the day. Originally I had asked to take the Monday before Thanksgiving off

We looked at the schedule of deadlines and he said, "If you want to do that, that's okay, but you have quarterly reports due the week you come back and then you need to start all the prep work for next year's upcoming data. It's going to be a lot."

Hmmm. "Okay, how about if I take the following Friday instead?"

He shook his head, "You have two reports due and emails to go with them. That's not a good idea." The emails he referred to were individual notes to every member in the sales group – which numbers upwards of seventy-five people. This is a monthly project that takes the better part of a day to complete. Yeah.

"Well how about *any* Monday or Friday between now and the end of the year?"

To that he replied that I had something due on each of those days – or that something "could" happen on one of those days. "Could" happen? Well shoot, the sky could come crashing down, couldn't it???

However, at the same time he says to me, "It's up to you. This is your call."

<u>Issue #2: My boss is an IDIOT</u>

Hold up a minute: If he's telling me that none of the days that I'm requesting are okay to take off, then this isn't my call... is it?

Okay. So then I told him that, if at all possible, I'd like a Monday or a Friday off. Who wouldn't want a long weekend, right?

Apparently that wasn't the right thing to say either. "Well," he started, "I'd like to have a long weekend too, Gabriel, but I realized that I had responsibilities to take care of so it forced me to take Tuesdays and Wednesdays instead."

Aside from the fact that I don't care, he has more vacation time each year to schedule. I don't deserve the grief over his inability to effectively plan his days off during the course of a year. After all, I only had one more vacation day to schedule out of the three weeks that I receive annually.

So I thought about it, looked at the schedule of deadlines and decided to suck it up. "Okay," I said, "why don't *you* tell me which Tuesday, Wednesday or Thursday is okay for me to take off."

He scanned through the schedule and shot down every last day between Thanksgiving and New Year's Eve. Of course he did. But then he followed that up with, "But it's up to you... it's your call."

So then I go back to the Monday before Thanksgiving. When I went back to this date, it went right back to the beginning of the conversation.

Do you see where this is going now? Good. Then please fill me in. I must have lost my roadmap."

Poor Gabriel.

Just Let Your Boss Be the Boss

Sometimes it's just easier to let it go than argue. Even though you may be completely right, it may completely stress you out to continually have to stand up for yourself (although, I understand, you must do this). Check out Ruth's story:

"My manager once gave me an assignment to update some training materials for some of our processes. Once completed, I'd have the opportunity to present the update to our sales department.

Those who know me know how much I enjoy creating and delivering presentations. When given the opportunity, I jump on it. Over the years several individuals had commented on my dynamic speaking presence. So, banging this presentation out was cake.

The day came to unveil the new and improved processes and I was fully prepared to deliver them. There was nothing unexpected that came up; no pregnant pauses, no misspeaking, no nervousness, nothing.

At the end of the dialogue, I fielded questions from those present. Since my manager also attended, she jumped in to answer most of them. Then the meeting broke up and we went back to our offices.

As I settled back in at my desk, my phone rang. It was my manager. She asked me to see her in her office. Okay.

On my way over there I'm thinking that she's going to compliment me on the smooth presentation - or at the very least thank me for completing the task so thoroughly.

So I go into her office and she asks me to close the door behind me. That's not usually a good sign. The only way that it would have been good is if she was offering me a raise or a promotion – and it had been far too long since both.

I take a seat and she glares at me from her side of the desk. "So," she starts, "how do you think the presentation went?"

I took a deep breath and thought about it for a few seconds and answered her, "I think it went very well."

Then she raised an eyebrow at me, "Oh really? You really thought that it was a good performance?"

Now I'm baffled... were we not in the same meeting? Of course I had to ask her, "Was something wrong with it? Did I make a mistake?" Now I'm wondering if I committed some horrible faux pas that I curiously missed.

She sighed and looked at me with an expression that

said, "How sad that you could be so stupid, you itty-bitty flea."

"Well, the presentation was all right," she said. "It just should have been better."

Excuse me?

"Okay, how could it have been better?" Should I have handed out lollipops at the end of it or raffled off a door prize for attending? I didn't get it.

"It could have been prepared better."

"Okay. What should I have done?" I asked. "Was there missing data? Unanswered questions?" I was really trying to understand what she was getting at.

"No, but I would have liked more time to review it before you presented it. I mean, you were making corrections to it up until thirty minutes before the meeting." Yeah, I was making corrections to it because you asked me to **BOLD** a word here, add a comma there... But none of the information needed to be altered because it was CORRECT. You sick, twisted control freak!

Under different circumstances, I might have been offended. However, when she told me that I stunk at the presentation I had to laugh. First of all, I've been doing this for a long time; I'm not a novice. I may not be the greatest writer ever but please don't tell me where to put my commas. Second, giving presentations is what I do.

She's obviously off her rocker. Although it would have been nice to have the recognition as warranted, I really couldn't take too much offense to this since she was so grossly off target."

THE MORAL TO THE STORY: Ruth's manager clearly felt the need to be a part of every little detail. It probably made her feel important. After all, she's "The Boss". At the end of the day, Ruth knows that her writing and presentation skills are competent enough for lots of other people. Just because her boss feels that way doesn't make it so! Most likely her bat-$#@%-crazy manager was simply jealous and needed something to nit-pick about. People like this shouldn't be working with humans. The best environment for her would be a basement in some far away place with all the oxygen sucked out of the room and the key lost forever.

Work Burnout

Work burnout is a condition that can leave you career-challenged. Once it has set in, it is very difficult to break free. Believe me, all the yoga in the world couldn't help me feel better about my job when I was still working. I tried all the suggestions that I read and took all kinds of advice from people. Nothing was going to help it because I couldn't get the cooperation needed to succeed. Of course, that was just my situation.

Signs of work burnout can be indicated by the presence of various symptoms. It can range from feeling overwhelmed, lack of energy and an inability to properly manage stress. People that experience work burnout tend to be pessimistic about their job and career path. They find it hard to relax and enjoy their time out of the office. When they're home, they're preoccupied with work. Some even have trouble sleeping and physical complaints.

These individuals are probably, under normal circumstances, excellent workers. However, their need to excel has caused them to take on too much work and responsibility. They become overwhelmed and are unable to focus. When they fail to live up to their expectations they become bitter, angry, and resentful.

Of course, there is something these people can do. They can approach their supervisors to work on setting realistic goals. That will work as long as their supervisor is not the one creating the issue in the first place. Other things they can do is to focus more on themselves by exercising, investigating options to relieve stress (though as I said, yoga did little for me… and I've been practicing for years), and finding other hobbies. Among other things, my personal favorite was to QUIT. This, of course, is my recommended course of action provided your manager will not work with you on alleviating your stress-related work factors. After all, too much stress leads to negative physical problems such as hypertension, heart disease, and weight gain.

It's funny now; I hear a lot of the same comments from people when I tell them that I've left my job. Usually, it's "Thank GOD you're finally out of there!!!" Looking back on the really bad times, it's crazy to think of what I went through. Remembering what it was like telling people almost felt as though they didn't always believe that what I was saying actually happened. It wasn't even supposed to go on for this long; everyone I spoke to was convinced I'd be out sooner. Unfortunately that wasn't the case… but that's not important now.

THE INCARCERATION IS OVER!

What's the point?

Sometimes root canal is more fun than going to work. For me, going to work at the end was really not fun. I was pushed and pushed and just couldn't take it anymore. I am not joking when I say that root canal was more fun for me than working in corporate America. Apart from the unfortunate financial expense of it, the root canal, the subsequent tooth infection and extraction, implant and crowing was incredibly more fun than dealing with this nonsense every day. I must have done something horrible in a past life to go through all of this now. Hopefully, I'm all paid up with Karma.

Lesson learned:

It doesn't matter what you do; if the job is going to suck, do what you must to survive it as long as you're going to be there. Murder is still illegal, so don't do it! Either get yourself fired or quit, or do what I did and start your own company!

CHAPTER TEN

Pretend It Didn't Happen

"People always say I didn't give up my seat because I was tired, but that isn't true. No, the only tired I was, was tired of giving in." - *Rosa Parks*

In Cahoots with My Dentist

Pretty much everyone I talked to knew my work situation. This went for my dentist as well.

My dentist isn't like other dentists I've known. He's a fast-talking, loud-mouthed New Yorker. Plus he's a joker. All things considered, my root canal was as pleasurable an experience as was possible. Then again, as I mentioned, having the root canal was more fun than working in corporate America.

Well, I told him and his assistant about my situation and how desperate I was for getting out. Like everyone else, they were horrified when I told them how long it was taking for me to find another job.

As I had also mentioned to everyone, I'd been job-hunting for almost eighteen months. I interviewed at every major competitor of my current company. The last place I interviewed with showed a great deal of promise. They called me back for four meetings. The last one was mid-morning one Thursday.

I came up with a good excuse to tell my manager so she wouldn't question me too hard about where I was going. I decided to tell her that I had a dental emergency involving the tooth that I was having the work on. Considering that I did have a few real emergencies with this tooth, it wasn't far-fetched. So I told my dentist about the excuse and he offered to write me a note for me to bring into work.

True to his word, he wrote the letter and printed it out on nice letterhead and placed it in an envelope. When I went back to work the morning of this interview, the story worked very well. I handed the note to my boss and not only did she not question me about my time out of the office, but she even commented on the nice letterhead.

I had accomplices far and wide who helped me to get out. I just wanted to share that little story with you.

Priceless

Southworth resume bond paper... $22.99 a box

Brand new suit from Ann Taylor... $249.00

Keeping it cool while the EVP of your current company catches you on an interview at the same office where he's scheduled a meeting with clients...

PRICELESS

Yes folks, that actually happened to me. Not only did I run into the EVP of my company, but also the SVP and a few other individuals. Incidentally, the SVP knew of my circumstance and was one of my job references.

So what a hoot – I ran into folks from my company and on probably the hottest day of the summer. What made it even more fun was that I had to wait in the reception area with all of them until we got called into our respective meetings. That was delightful.

When my interviewer came out to greet me (thankfully it was after the others had gone into their meeting), he commented on the weather. "Wow, it's a real scorcher out there isn't it? I'll bet you were really sweating it out on your way over."

"Well Mr. Interviewer, funny you should mention that. I would have to say it was more of a scorcher in your reception area. I ran into half a dozen people from my office there."

He apologized, laughed and then turned me down for the job. Life can be so cruel. But no – to my knowledge these individuals did not share my faux pas with the loony upper-management powers that be in my department. I'm willing to bet that they were secretly rooting for me.

It's a funny story though – and completely true. Trust me when I say that material this good just could not be made up. Entertained yet? Good, then you got your money's worth. I knew people would like that story. Even me. It still cracks me up.

Who knows, maybe I have some wisdom from all this that I can impart to others along my journey.

Open Call for Idiot Bosses: National Idiot Boss Association Membership Drive for 2006

Don't be left out in the cold! With the new year fast approaching, now is the time to join the National Idiot Boss Association – or to renew your previous membership.

About Us: Founded in 2004, NIBA consists of a rag-tag group of micro-managers, bullies, control freaks, headmaster-managers (the grammar-freaks), dictator-managers, and generally imbalanced morons with massive self esteem issues.

NIBA's mission: To provide a forum for sucking the life out of everyone that works for you and for promoting the most unprofessional managerial styles known to man; to serve as a catalyst for the displacement of bright and motivated individuals in all aspects of business; to promote and support malevolent endeavors through the NIBA Foundation.

WHAT WE DO: Through various, dedicated managerial "slaughter house" committees, NIBA holds about 365 events per year (after all, most of us work weekends as we expect our staff to do. We do not support any semblance of family life and recommend a ritual sacrifice of each member's firstborn (or family pet)). We do not promote Work-Life balance. If you do, then go hug a tree; we don't want you. Each of our hackneyed programs aims to devalue career skills and push back current industry trends at least 40 or so years. If you stink at what you do, confuse, derail and demean your staff at every opportunity, then this association is for you.

Sign up now!!! And don't forget to bring a friend (if you have any, that is).

NIBA's next calendar event:
January 11 – Boardroom Breakfast
I.M. AMORON, CEO Murders and Executions, New York City
The Morningstar Times Building
The 7th Circle of Hell
(1/4 of a mile west of the river Styx)
Mismanagement Weekly recently called him...
"The most debasing man in business, and one of the dumbest."
We can all learn something from him.
NIBA will salute those traits and many more as members of the bad-business-practices and micro-management community "Roast and Toast I.M. AMORON."

<u>The EXIT Interview</u>

(What we'd love to say when we quit)

If you were the head of your department, what would you do differently to make everyone more productive? How would you run the business?

Motivated employees are a key part to any company's success. If people are properly motivated, companies stand to gain enormous results from almost nothing. Company X has the resources and capabilities to provide this to their employees.

One way to do this is to implement employee enrichment programs between various departments. Another good motivational tool that works is "cross-training" to be available to those employees that request it. Although I don't believe that the department I worked in fostered a warm or social environment, I think this effort would allow anyone interested to know what the department is about and explore all aspects of it. I know other companies integrate this into their employee-motivation programs and have success with it. I think you would benefit from it as well.

Employees should also expect to be motivated by their managers. I know of managers that could profit from learning how to properly motivate their staff. There is no quicker way to de-motivate people than by micromanaging. Specifically, I mean things like nit-picking about how to structure an email subject header, which font to use and the like. Another thing that deflates a person's self-esteem is to repeatedly point the finger and throw blame – whether rightfully so or not.

Again, managers I've had in the past managed this way and it showed. Let's take a look at a team I worked on a while back: I.M.Happytobegone – my predecessor in my final role at Company X – made it very clear upon her departure what the conditions were like when she reported to Manager Clueless. I.M. left the company because of these conditions.

Subordinate A and Subordinate B were both fairly new when they reported to Manager Clueless. Due to the massive breakdown in communication and lack of positive reinforcement they should have received from her, they became disillusioned and their performances reflected exactly how they felt: lackluster. Their poor work was then blamed on I.M. who had no manager and no direction for the first few months of her employment (which only lasted a year anyway). Subordinate A and B trained I.M. because there was no one else available to do so. Yet Manager Clueless and her boss scratched their heads and wondered what happened.

Why is that?

If you could add or change a benefit at Company X, what would it be?

One topic that continues to come up everywhere is telecommuting. At Headquarters, this may be a commonplace practice, but where I worked it's a very different story. I've worked in departments where it seemed as though certain individuals received preferential treatment when it came to this benefit. Granted, not every job can be done from the comfort of one's home. It's a given that the individual's role needs to have the flexibility present to take advantage of this benefit.

However, I saw evidence of this treatment on the occasions of inclement weather as well as during the New York City transit strike. There were those that had permission to work from home; though not as many as should have been allowed. Friends of mine (who worked in other companies) who were allowed to work from home had much different work situations than mine. Plus, they were trusted by their management. It just felt like certain individuals were able to take advantage of this benefit while others weren't. And I'm not talking about those present being the skeleton crew. A skeleton crew makes sense. But I didn't see this. There seemed to be little rhyme or reason behind it. Why was that?

Right around that time, I was suffering from a severe tooth infection (which incidentally was extracted in an emergency procedure on that first day of the strike) and was on painkillers (as management was aware). But at 6 a.m., I was on my way to the office and I was there early. I was legitimately sick but made my way in (I'm sure no one would have believed it if I called out on that day!). However, as I mentioned, others had the luxury of working from home.

This telecommuting policy needs to be scrutinized a little more.

What is the best thing about your job?

If you asked me that question four years ago, I would have been able to provide a list of things as long as my arm.

Today, my answer is "going home".

Say Goodnight, Gracie

In the spirit of Resignation, I decided to share something with you. You know how some websites have those fun little quizzes that you can take to show you how smart you are, or romantic, or adventurous? Well I found one on Kissmyfreckledassbye.com to determine if I should quit my job (by the way, this was before I quit my job).

Here's what it said in response to my answers:

"You should definitely quit your job. You're using your job as an excuse not to do what you are really meant to. Obviously, who you are and what you do are solidly connected in your mind. Chances are your very spirit is entrepreneurial, or you have a deep- seated disrespect for all authority, or you have to do something that is eating at you for your neglect of it. Quit already. Go, start your own company, write the novel, paint the picture. People like you, at your stage of life really shouldn't be working for anyone else."

Hmmmm.

Ciao For Now

So what do you do once you've tendered your resignation?

I used to get all giddy when I thought about leaving my job. I played out in my head all the possible scenarios of what it would be like when I finally left. Here are some things you need to be aware of before your final departure.

Purge

The first thing you do is purge all personal files that you may have on your desktop. I'd delete any/all non-work-related emails and even delete the cookies. The less you leave behind, the better. Come to think of it, you may want to do this before you submit your resignation. In the event that you are immediately escorted out of the building, you will lose any opportunity to "clean up".

Free Escort Service

Not everyone has the pleasure of being escorted out of the building. If you work with proprietary information or go to work for a competitor, the company may be uncomfortable about you staying. Otherwise, you'll most likely remain for the standard two weeks.

"It's not you, it's me"

Don't feel bullied to cite your reasons for leaving or where you're going. That should really be up to you and what you're comfortable with. You should be able to get by with, "I'm sorry to be leaving the company but am looking forward to a new opportunity/challenge." It behooves you to avoid negativity. That old adage is true: You really never know who you'll run into down the road. You may need a reference. Crazier things have happened. It will make you look better if you keep your mouth shut and don't give in to saying how you may REALLY feel.

Then again, it may make you feel a lot better to say what's really on your mind. I no longer feel that there is necessarily a "right" way and a "wrong" way to resign. It may be better for your karma to take the high road, but who says that you can't tell Inhuman Resources that, "You know why I'm leaving? Because the staff that runs my department is shabby at best. I was treated better by the bully on the playground when I was eight." Thanks for playing, goodbye.

The Exit Interview

Don't feel compelled to do one!!! I know, I know, you *should* go along, be polite and submit to one. If you choose to do so, it's good to say that you're simply leaving for a better opportunity. Bottom line, this is the reason that most people leave anyway. However, the way I see it is this: If I'm leaving because I'm miserable (and that would be me), why would I want to talk to HR now? If they didn't want to listen to me when I needed them, why should I help them? Chances are, nothing will be done about any grievances since it would really be "a day late and a buck short". Don't bother.

On the other hand, you can go to the other extreme and let it all out – diplomatically, of course.

When Mary was getting ready to leave her unhappy job, she decided that she didn't want to go too quietly. She not only agreed to do an exit interview, but she sent her written answers to Inhuman Resources with copies to the executive administration in the corporate office, as well as a copy to the president of the company. Whether anything ever came of her insights on the goings-on of her former department and boss, she never knew. However, Mary felt better knowing that she at least did what she could to enlighten those that most likely had no idea what was going on. She felt that she did her part.

The exit interview is really up to the individual.

Two Weeks' Notice

You are not required to offer more notice than this (unless you are under some prior contractual agreement). Of course, this is up to you as well. If you'd like to extend your stay until say, a replacement is found, you can certainly volunteer it.

It's also your prerogative to leave and never come back, though I wouldn't personally recommend it. That will just make you look bad. Besides, your intention to screw your boss over may backfire when your unfinished work is then dumped on your former colleagues' desk. They won't appreciate it.

Do You Really Want to Resign "Diplomatically"?

I read an article the other day that offered various suggestions on how to resign diplomatically. Before I get into this, I just have to say that this should really be fairly obvious. Unless you're young and have no corporate experience, most of this should really be common sense.

Once a resignation is tendered there are some important things to remember. The first thing is that you may be escorted out of the building.

The next thing to be aware of is being guilted by your boss or co-workers. It's possible that others may be envious of your new move. They may even attempt to make you feel as though you're deserting them. The thing to focus on here is your own responsibility to your job. It's important to wrap up any projects you may be working on or training your replacement. The key is to remain positive.

Of course it's entirely possible that you will receive no response whatsoever. This happened to me. Not only was no one surprised to hear my news, it was expected and unbelievably, something that my manager wanted to facilitate ("Don't let the door hit your ass on the way out..."). I think they really wanted me to go! So, while I know it's important to be diplomatic, I will not play by someone else's "rules" just because they say they know better. Only I can be the judge of that.

Another thing to think about is what to do should you receive a counteroffer. It hasn't been often in my career that I've heard others receiving counters, but I suppose it is possible. If you're in a bad situation, don't eliminate the chance of being walked out. I had to stay for my two weeks. Of course, they may do this to get whatever they can out of you before you go.

In that case, it's important to remember that you can only do so much. You can't be expected to do it all before your departure. It would probably be nice, though, to help where you can since the responsibilities may fall to those you don't want to see tortured. It can be a hard thing to do, but think about if the tables were turned. If you've been on the receiving end of that, you'll know what I mean. Then, if the situation is so god-awful that you can't stand it any longer, then you have my permission to do what you need to do in order to survive.

The other thing to think about in regards to a counteroffer is that it may end up hurting you. For starters, studies show that the majority of people that accept counteroffers don't stay long with the job. It puts your loyalty in question. If you'll "so easily" be ready to go, it may destroy any remaining trust. Be very careful with this one.

The last thing I want to bring up is the exit interview. I know, I know, you've heard me moan about this before. I used to think there was no point in giving one since the chances of any positive action going into effect as a result was slim to none. However, my personal feeling is that if there's something you feel very strongly about then by all means, submit to one and state the facts. In order to remain credible it's important to stay unattached. Don't whine and complain randomly. State things as they are, plus some suggestions as to how to make things better. Of course the other option is to remain positive.

At the end of the day the way you go out is really up to you. It's true you never know who you'll run into down the road or what favor/recommendation you may need. Personally, I pushed all that advice aside. My management was the reason I left a particular job and I had no problems going to the top of the corporate hierarchy to let them know it. There was no way I was going back for any references; I simply did not respect them enough to think they'd be important to someone else. I've known many people over the course of my career that I'm sure would go to bat for me. After all, I did have a solid reputation. Again, I only speak for myself on this one.

Before doing anything, be sure you've thought things through and weighed the advantages and possible consequences. If you've done that and still want to let it all out, then good luck to you.

THE GREATEST RESIGNATION LETTER EVER

The following resignation letter is REAL. I've only altered it so company/department/industry names have been changed.

This letter is from someone I know. As a matter of fact, it's someone that I used to work with at the company referred to in the letter. Even better than that - this letter was written to Inhuman Resources and the manager in question is none other than one I had worked for at a later time (though not willingly). That's right, the author of this letter was my predecessor in this role.

Anyway, on with the letter. I hope you enjoy it as much as I did. The author is my hero, the wind beneath my wings.

To Whom It May Concern:

Let this serve as my official letter of resignation from Company X as of July 15, 2004. It actually makes me sad to have to leave such a wonderful organization as Company X. I joined this company with the hope, anticipation and excitement of learning a great deal from such an industry leader, when instead my time here in Department X has been anything BUT rewarding. When I arrived here my immediate boss was on a leave of absence with no indication of where she was or when she would return. I felt it left me with no guidance as a new manager and made it difficult to run a team of three analysts. I credit my analysts for stepping up and teaching me all the day-to-day responsibilities of the team.

Having seven years in this industry, I have never seen such a lack of communication between the upper management and their subordinates. I feel that Miss Manager is never clear cut with her answers and is often vague about many situations. This department often leaves their employees in the dark, which causes a very negative & stressful atmosphere about what will occur next. This is not an environment which allows you to grow and expand professionally, therefore a place I do NOT want to be a part of.

I have learned over the years that a good manager must build solid relationships with their employees in order to gain respect and foster positive working conditions. I consider myself an extremely diligent & hard worker that always gives 110 percent. However, when there is no respect present, I am unmotivated and unwilling to go that extra mile.

Working under Miss Manager did not allow me room for autonomy as a manager, due to her MICROSCOPIC management skills. In my time here at Company X, I felt that I haven't learned anything more than I already knew. Instead, I felt like an English teacher correcting emails and a babysitter, rather than an industry professional.

Therefore, due to the poor management skills of my supervisor Miss Manager and for the reasons mentioned above, I've chosen to terminate my employment with Company X.

Sincerely,
I.M. Happytobegone

The Resignation

Getting a new job can be exciting. But before you start downing the celebratory cocktails, there's one necessary item that needs to be addressed: The Resignation Letter. Most people will advise (myself included) that it's important to keep things professional and to the point. In most cases, you don't want to burn bridges because you really never know if you'll cross paths again or if you need a reference.

The standard resignation letter should include the following information:

- State your intention to resign
- Share your reason (totally optional)… relocation, acceptance of another offer, you can't stand to be there for a second longer, etc.
- Mention two weeks' notice as a professional courtesy
- Indicate the final date of employment
- Include a "thank you" to the employer for the opportunity to work for the organization (again, totally optional)

The letter can be written just to state the facts or include (as professionally as possible) the reason(s) for the departure.

Another option for you to consider is:

"Dear So-and-So:

I quit.

May the Force be with you,
Employee X"

The $64,000 Question

Since the big day (my last day in Corporate Hell), I've had many people asking the following questions:

1. How did the resignation meeting go?

2. How do I feel?

My answers:

#1: "The Meeting" lasted less than five minutes. Since my managers were both out on vacation, I had to go above their heads. That was a treat. I handed my resignation to my boss' boss' boss. She wasn't surprised in the least. But if you think about it, who would be? Everyone around me knew my situation – there was no doubt in anyone's mind *why* I was going.

Of course, everyone wanted to know where I was headed. I didn't say a word until after I was gone. I wanted to keep that information to myself.

#2: I feel fine. Actually, I feel more or less the same way I did before I resigned. Although I'm anxious and scared of the uncertainty that my future holds, not once did it occur to me not to resign. This was something that I knew had to be done. It's that simple.

Finale

My last day of employment in corporate America was not marked by celebrations, dancing, tequila shots or anything merry.

As I walked out, I felt disappointment. The system that I thought believed in me as I so naively believed in it many years ago disappointed me. I thought that after so long with the company, my managers would see me off with congratulations and well wishes. I was sorry when that was not the case.

My departure was anticlimactic. Since it was a holiday weekend many people were already gone. I picked up my belongings (sorry, no trophy) and walked out the door. Before I reached the elevator my manager came to say good-bye and disappeared quick. That was it. No "good luck", no "It's been nice knowing you". Nothing.

I can't say I'm surprised by that, although I am disappointed. I'm disappointed too that neither of her two managers had so much as two words to say to me during my last two weeks. These are people I reported to for several years.

So people want to know how great it feels to finally put that place behind me. Did I boogie on out? Did I party till the sun came up? No.

Although I left with no regrets, I did leave with a hefty amount of anger, hurt and resentment. I know in time I'll put it all behind me, but that last day... well, it wasn't what I expected.

When I got home I was so exhausted I slept for a few hours; it was the end of a very, very, very long day.

Cheered by the Busload

It happened time and again that I would have terrifying dreams about work. Especially in my last job.

Last night however, I had a dream that I was sitting on a bench at a bus stop. It was a warm sunny day. There was someone to my right who I didn't know. Then a woman approached and sat on the end of the bench next to this other person. It was a VP from my office.

At that point a yellow school bus pulled up to the bus stop. The driver opened the door and people started to hang out of the bus and out of the windows. They were people I'd worked with over the past several years at my last job. It took me a moment to notice that they were cheering loudly. It took me another moment to realize that they were cheering for me. This busload of former colleagues was fully behind me and supportive. They were ecstatic.

It made me feel wonderful.

Then I looked to the right to see if Ms. VP was still there and she was... looking the other way. Not once did she acknowledge this boisterous crowd cheering me on. How typical. But you know, it was okay. Certain opinions never mattered much to me anyway. I just thought the dream was cool.

When the Boss is a Coward

There are many unpleasant things we endure when we work for someone else. Of course, there is the rare occasion where we actually like our jobs and our bosses, but for the most part, people either simply put up with it or are flat-out miserable.

Most times, you know what kind of person you're dealing with when it comes to your boss. If you've been in your job long enough, you know who your boss is and the things that make them tick.

If you're lucky, your boss is a good, intelligent, and wise leader. They'll be upfront about your strengths and weaknesses and let you know where you stand almost all of the time.

If you're unlucky you won't see any of that. You'll constantly be in the dark about what's happening, what your boss is doing and even what it is you're supposed to be doing.

But the truly unlucky are people such as myself, who have had bosses that possess a natural look of a deer in headlights. If there is such a thing as a "natural" look as this, these people have it.

Here's an example of what I mean by this: you were given a project that's been changed over and over so that you no longer have any idea what the objective is. On top of that, you're being criticized and you don't know why since you're only following the last set of orders given. Then, to rub salt in the wound, when the boss yells at you and you ask why, they say NOTHING.

A good boss will tell you the answer. A bad boss will lie to your face. The ultimate in idiot bosses will simply stare at you. No words, no nothing. Just a blank stare. There's no better way to send the signal of "we don't want you here" than by not giving any response when one is requested.

In my book, this is cowardice. If you don't like the job that I'm doing, it is your responsibility as my manager to tell me so that I can fix it. If you tell me nothing it makes you a bad boss with no spine.

Go find a book. Read it to get a clue; then steal the spine and attach it to your back. It may be temporary, but you'll get the feel for what having one is really like.

What's the point?

Two things:

1. Getting fired isn't the end of the world.
2. You can always quit.

Lesson learned:

This chapter is clearly all about gettin' the hell outta Dodge. Everyone has their limits. If you've honestly given your job the good 'ol college try and nothing has worked, then it's time to go. Seriously. As I said in my Introduction, I do not claim to have the answers as many authors do. I'm not sure that there are answers.

Results are largely dependent upon who you work with. Try as you may, you will never be able to change others. It may be possible to work out the occasional compromise, but stupid bosses will always be stupid. It's best to know how to protect yourself while still doing what you were hired to do. If you can no longer do that and your reputation, as well as your sanity is hanging in the balance, then it's time to cut your losses and move on.

Epilogue

My journey was an educational one. It was emotional and volatile too, but I learned a lot from my experiences.

It's unfortunate though, that I am unable to provide clear-cut answers to the great questions of how to deal with difficult bosses and co-workers. However, I saw from my experiences that I had something to share with others. My story is hardly that unique. But when I shared my stories, people really listened because they *related* to what I was saying. Everyone has evil boss stories. Mine just pushed me into a new career, which is the greatest thing that could have happened to me.

As I made my way toward self-employment, I learned valuable lessons. My departure from the corporate life was not without its rewards. I learned how to:

Perfect a resume.
Ace tough interview questions.
Mentor college students and junior employees.
Say the "right" things.
Build a new business.
Write and publish a book.
Start a new career.
Hone my networking skills.

I just woke up one day and knew I couldn't do "the corporate thing" anymore. I'd read so many books and articles by individuals claiming to have the answers but didn't. It's really tough; only by trial and error is anyone going to know how to handle their situation. It may happen that someone will be helped by this information, but ultimately there is no single piece of advice I could leave for anyone other than this: Protect yourself. If you can no longer do that, then get out. If you cannot get out then do what you can while you are trying to get out. Don't be so afraid of your future. Some of the most successful people in business have been fired or pushed out of other jobs. There are many, many options out there.

If nothing else, I just hope these tales have entertained. Entertaining is certainly a word I can use now that I'm not in those situations anymore.

Good luck to you.

Bibliography

"10 Tips for Performing Under Pressure". CARS Group International. http://www.carsgroup.com/Online-Jobs-NewsLetter-53.html, (February, 2006).

Adams, Scott. The Dilbert Principle. New York: HarperCollins Publishers, Inc., 1997.

"Are You Burning Out?". iVillage. http://quiz.ivillage.com/uk_work/tests/burnout.htm, (April, 2006).

"Definitions of Insubordination". Google. http://www.google.com/search?hl=en&lr=&pwst=1&defl=en&q=define:insubordination&sa=X&oi=glossary_definition&ct=title, (June, 2006).

Elgin, Suzette Haden, Ph.D. The Gentle Art of Verbal Self-Defense at Work. New Jersey: Prentice Hall Press, 2000.

Flanigan, James and Mulligan, Thomas S. "Peter Drucker Passes On". Interesting-People Message. http://www.interesting-people.org/archives/interesting-people/200511/msg00182.html, (July, 2006).

"Forty-Three Percent of Workers Called in Sick With Fake Excuses in the Last 12 Months, CareerBuilder.com's Survey Finds". Careerbuilder. http://www.careerbuilder.com/share/aboutus/pressreleasesdetail.aspx?id=pr195&sd=10/4/2005&ed=12/31/2005, (April, 2006).

Fulghum, Robert. All I Really Need to Know I Learned in Kindergarten. New York: Random House, Inc., 1986.

Green, Thad. "Create an Environment That Promotes Confidence, Trust and Satisfaction to Motivate Employees". Northern Arizona University. http://hr.nau.edu/content/ newsletters/aug03/, (May, 2006).

Hansen, Randall S., Ph.D. "Resigning With Class: How to Diplomatically Resign From Your Job". Quintessential Careers. http://www.quintcareers.com/resigning_job.html, (April, 2006).

Heathfield, Susan M. "Performance Management Process Checklist". About. http://humanresources.about.com/od/ performancemanagement/a/perfmgmt.htm, (December, 2005).

Hochheiser, Robert M. Its a Job Not a Jail: How to Break Your Shackles When You Cant Afford to Quit. New York: Fireside, 1998.

Horn, Sam. Take the Bully by the Horns. New York: St. Martin's Press. 2002.

"Insubordination". itssimple.biz. http://www.itssimple.biz/biz_ tools/text/P05_5330.html, (June, 2006).

Lorenz, Kate. "Can You Redeem Yourself After a Bad Review at Work?". City of Sacramento. http://216.239.51.104/ search?q=cache:dcYr2Etgo40J:www.cityofsacramento.org/od/ Images/CityToolboxJan06_P4.pdf+kate+lorenz+Can+You+Red eem+Yourself+After+a+Bad+Review+at+Work%3F&hl=en&gl= us&ct=clnk&cd=1, (December, 2005).

Lorenz, Kate. "Eight Signs Your Job is Doomed". Careerbuilder.com. http://msn.careerbuilder.com/Custom/ MSN/CareerAdvice/541.htm?siteid=cbmsnmm4426&sc_ extcmp=JS_wi3_may05_mymsn&cbRecursionCnt=1&cbsid=45 eb26ade1d2486eb4e7a85ac534f4c8-181122037-to-1, (November, 2005).

Lorenz, Kate. "Ten Attitudes of Successful Workers". The Career Place. http://thecareerplace.berkeley.edu/tip0306.htm, (March, 2006).

Lorenz, Kate. "When You Love Your Job But Hate Your Boss". Careerbuilder.com. http://msn.careerbuilder.com/custom/msn/careeradvice/viewarticle.aspx?articleid=773&SiteId=cbms nch4773&sc_extcmp=JS_773_msn&cbRecursionCnt=1&cbsid =2fb8aecb00354272bb89e85bc6a9e4de-209419871-X3-2, (June, 2006).

Lubit, Roy H, M.D., Ph.D. Coping with Toxic Managers, Subordinates... and Other Difficult People. New Jersey: Financial Times Prentice Hall, 2004.

"Management Bullies Require Attention". Badbossology. http://www.badbossology.com/i4789-c45-email, (June, 2006).

"Micromanage". The Free Dictionary by Farlex. http://www.thefreedictionary.com/micromanager, (April, 2006).

Persaud, Raj, M.D. Staying Sane. United Kingdom: Bantam Books, 2001.

Richardson, Bradley G. Career Comeback. New York: Random House, Inc., 2004.

Spencer, Johnson, M.D. Who Moved My Cheese?. New York: Penguin Putnam Inc., 1998.

"The Dangers of Being a Micromanager". AllBusiness. http://www.allbusiness.com/employment/management/11235, (May, 2006).

"The Kiss Off Quiz". Kiss My Freckled Ass Goodbye. http://www.kissmyfreckledassbye.com/quiz.html, (February, 2006).

"Those Who Can Do, Those Who Can't, Bully". Bully Online. http://www.bullyonline.org/workbully/manage.htm, (February, 2006).

"Tick Life Cycle and Habits". Do-It-Yourself Pest Control. http://www.pestproducts.com/ticks1.htm, (May, 2006).

"What People Want to Say to the Boss". Toxic Boss. http://toxicboss.com/saytoboss/index.html, (January, 2006).

"What's Your Excuse?". Duct Tape Guy. http://www.octanecreative.com/Parodyville/excuses/, (April, 2006).

Willis, Gerri. "How to Manage Your Manager". CNN. http://money.cnn.com/2005/03/16/pf/saving/willis_tips/index.htm, (March, 2005).

"Word Origins, Workaholic". Answers.com. http://www.answers.com/topic/workaholic, (April, 2006).

Made in the USA